Reagan's Terrible Swift Sword

Reforming & Controlling
the
Federal Bureaucracy

Donald J. Devine

Jameson Books, Inc.
Ottawa, Illinois

Jameson Books, Inc. titles are distributed to the book
trade by National Book Network, Lanham, Maryland.

Customers desiring Jameson books at special
discounts for bulk purchases, sales promotions,
premiums, fundraising, or educational use, should
write the publisher at:

Jameson Books, Inc.
722 Columbus Street
Ottawa, Illinois 61350
815-434-7905; FAX 434-7907
Printed in the United States of America
ISBN: 0-89803-163-X

Library of Congress Cataloging-in-Publication Data

Devine, Donald John, 1937–
Reagan's terrible swift sword : reforming & controlling
the federal bureaucracy / Donald J. Devine.
p. cm.

Includes index.
ISBN 0–89803-163-X
1. Civil service—United States—Personnel
management. 2. Civil service—United States. 3.
Bureaucracy—United States. 4. United States—Politics
and government—1981–1989. I. Title.
JK765.D48 1990   91–29883
353/001—dc20   CIP

5 4 3 2 1 91 92 93 94 95

Contents

Preface

It's always hard to say no, especially in politics. Our founders knew this, and tried to create a government whose leaders could say no to bad laws and ruinous spending. Even so, few people can get elected by saying no to too many people or organized interests. But government needs politicians who say no, no matter how difficult this is, if self government is to survive. It was this defect in human nature that led Aristotle to believe democracies could not survive very long.

America's founders constructed a government that made it more difficult to say yes. They divided powers between the states and the national government, they separated the national power into three branches, and left all the powers not delegated to the governments in the hands of the people themselves. The president was given the specific authority to say no to the legislative branch—that one most likely to say yes to special interests—through the power called the veto. Our founders' structure lasted a long time, until Woodrow Wilson figured out how to consolidate the power to say yes behind the very person who was supposed to say no, the president.

But the founders also said that part of the government must say yes, the executive branch. For that was to be its active, energetic force, balanced by the others. Having executives say yes to their duty is difficult too; especially so because of the checking powers of the other branches. This book tells the story of how an administration tried to go back to the founders' tradition of saying both no to special interests and yes to the need for change. It also unfolds my own story specifically about reforming government management. I wish to dedicate it to all those in the Reagan administration who had the courage to say no to the interests and yes to responsibility, beginning with President Reagan himself and five top officials who were remarkably able: James Watt, Raymond Donovan, James Miller, Gerald Carmen, and Thomas Pauken. A very few at the White House, particularly Becky Norton Dunlop, Willa Ann Johnson, and Kenneth Cribb, also knew how to say no and when to say yes. At the U.S. Office of Personnel Management (the civil service), we had a good team: especially, George Nesterczuk, James Burns, Terry Culler, Michael Frost, Patrick Korten, Robert Moffit, Joseph Morris, James Morrison, Mary Rose, Mark Tapscott, Clifford White, George Woloshyn, and Michael Sanera.

Most important, I want to applaud the following elected legislators, because for them to say no took special courage. Saying no cost many of them their jobs. During my tenure at OPM, there was only one recorded vote where senators were allowed to vote yes or no for good government management, a fact which itself says much about the importance Congress gives to management issues. The vote was on whether to extend the idea of pay for performance to the government's white collar work force. There was no real argument over the merits; everyone believed in theory that we should move pay from being based upon simple seniority to being based more upon performance. Still, only eighteen senators had the intestinal fortitude to say no to the civil service pressure groups. They were: Jeremiah Denton,

Pete Wilson, William Armstrong, Mack Mattingly, Jim McClure, Steve Symms, Dick Lugar, Roger Jepsen, Bob Dole, Ed Zorinsky, Chic Hecht, Paul Laxalt, Gordon Humphrey, Warren Rudman, John East, Jesse Helms, Jim Abdnor, and Malcolm Wallop. Only one was a Democrat, Senator Zorinsky. Of the Republicans, five (Armstrong, East, Humphrey, Laxalt, and McClure) did not seek reelection, and five lost their next election: Denton, Mattingly, Jepsen, Abdnor, and Hecht. Quite a record for saying no to bureaucratic interests on such a commonsense bill. The good ones mostly leave in frustration or get defeated.

The major thesis of this book is that government is political; and in order for it to be managed effectively, it must be organized and administered according to political principles. Government is neither business administration nor campaign management, although it borrows principles from each. Best illustrating this, perhaps, is an incident from the second term of the Reagan administration, otherwise beyond the purview of this book.

Since the time of Woodrow Wilson, those who have believed in his theory of nonpolitical administration of government have asked for two reforms that they claimed would lead to better and more efficient government: an executive branch which was, (1) centralized in a presidency composed of powerful White House staff offices to mobilize Congress and the bureaucracy to carry out the president's mandate; and (2) staffed by a professional bureaucracy that followed neutral rather than political principles of administration, with leadership provided by career civil servants rather than by political appointees. Both principles foundered upon the Iran-Contra affair. This one major blunder of the Reagan administration was the fruit of a central White House staff office led by career officials.

The critical fact was that an advisory staff agency, the National Security Council, was given a mission that could only have been successfully performed by a fully staffed and supported line agency. Congress, in a fit of micromanagement, forbade the line agencies—including the one which should have carried out the mission, the Central Intelligence Agency— to become involved, and the nearly inevitable result in such a delicate situation was the failure that eventually happened. This was compounded by placing military officers in charge of the operation. We should not expect career civil servants in staff agencies not under direct political supervision to prosecute such sensitive operations; and when we then convict them, we simply add insensitivity to error. When we place neutral officers in such positions, we are unfairly asking them to perform functions in which they are not experienced.

It is no coincidence that most of the successful presidencies preceded the powerful staff agencies in the White House Office and the Executive Office of the President (especially the Office of Management and Budget and the National Security Council). These White House staff institutions were invented in the early twentieth century to manage the new "welfare state," but they did not dominate the process until the late 1940s. Even down to Dwight Eisenhower, cabinet government was still the way to run the national government—which meant that the line agencies, headed by politically sensitive appointees, ran the regular operations of government. Since Eisenhower, the White House staff has dominated the cabinet, with the result that no administration since then has functioned effectively—with one president resigning, one without the political support to run for a second term, one dying in office after three frustrating and generally unsuccessful years in power, and two not elected to a second term—until the Reagan administration.

As our national government grew to enormous size and power, the agency bureaucracies took on lives of their own, usually representing the interests they were supposed to regulate. In response, the central management agencies were made even stronger, to give the president leverage. In the course of time, this reliance upon White House staff became an excuse not to staff the executive branch with the type of cabinet and political leaders needed to control the bureaucracies.

The result was constant warfare between the White House and the agencies and further increases in central management agencies' operations and oversight as the process became more and more complex and inefficient.

The president himself and his top aides in the White House simply do not have the time or enough trusted political staffs to manage complex line-agency operations. Congress doesn't either. Only the line agencies in the cabinet and subcabinet have the resources, actual and potential. Unless a political team with the necessary loyalty is built in the agencies, no president can provide effective leadership over a sprawling bureaucracy. It was this belief that underlay the personnel management theory that I attempted to implement in the first Reagan administration. How to make government, especially its bureaucracy, responsible to the people through political leadership is the problem of democratic government today, and is the subject to which we now turn.

I would like to thank Caroline Fiel for her assistance in preparing this manuscript; William Bowen, Paul Farago, Fred Lennon, and Ron Robinson for their encouragement; Jameson Campaigne for his invaluable editing, advice, and support; Richard Nathan, Aaron Wildavsky, and Joseph Morris for reading the manuscript and for suggestions; and my wife, Ann, and our children, William, Michael, Patricia, and Joseph, for the sustenance that made my time in government worthwhile and this book possible.

1

Reagan's Terrible Swift Sword

The Sunday magazine headline "Reagan's Terrible Swift Sword of the Civil Service" sums up what the *Washington Post* thought of my tenure as head of the federal government's bureaucracy. In its national edition, I was pictured as Che Guevara (beret and all) and described as conducting "war on the civil service."

A *Post* columnist said that I was the best-known head of the civil service since Theodore Roosevelt, but also styled me as "combative." For Christmas, the *New York Times* called me "the Grinch," which the Associated Press embellished as "Grinch in a Pin-Striped Suit." My favorite was "Devine, Rasputin of the Reduction in Force."

What caused all of this?

Ronald Reagan said it was because I "took on with vigor and determination one of the toughest, but most important challenges we faced when we assumed office. [Devine] faced this vital task with steadiness of purpose and accomplished it with both character and compassion." My success in managing the government's two million employees "can be measured in billions of dollars in budget savings achieved," according to President Reagan.

A totally different picture was painted by the federal employee unions and associations: they considered me Public Enemy Number One. Likewise, congressmen and senators with large government employee constituencies were unhappy with my performance. Indeed, given my commitment to the president's promise to cut government, I obviously would win few friends as head of the civil service in its company town. But, then, I took comfort in President Truman's immortal words, "If you need a friend in Washington, buy a dog." So I bought two to be on the safe side, and entered upon a wonderful adventure of helping the president try to make the government work.

President Reagan began by telling me what he wanted me to do. We were to freeze new hiring, we were to cut the number of nondefense positions in government, we were to subject employee benefits and other programs to budget scrutiny, we were to make federal employees work harder with fewer resources, and we were to establish policy control over the bureaucracy. The mission was to make the bureaucracy respond to his new political mandate; and this inevitably would create waves.

But presidents have tried to get control of the bureaucracy before. John F. Kennedy once lined up fourteen people in the Oval Office and went systematically down the chain of command, starting with the person to whom he had originally given an order to find out why it had not been carried out. He never learned the answer.

Franklin D. Roosevelt put it this way:

> The Treasury is so large and far-flung and ingrained in its practices that I find it almost impossible to get the actions and results I want—even with Henry [Morgenthau, my best person] there. But the Treasury is not to be compared with the State Department. You should go through the experience

of trying to get changes in the thinking, policies, and actions of career diplomats and then you'd know what a real problem was. But the Treasury and State Department put together are nothing compared with the Navy.

President Reagan was not unprepared for the difficulty he faced. He had been a two-term governor. And frustration with civil-service regulations when he was a personnel officer at Culver City during World War II opened his eyes. He found that he could not fire an incompetent who worked for him because of the rigidity of civil service procedures. He learned that government operated differently from the private sector, and much less efficiently.

There is no question that government is different. The essential difference is that the government bureaucracies do not have markets, or profit and loss bottom lines to make them subject to consumer discipline. A large corporation can be successful because it operates in a competitive market, whose bottom line profit and loss signals to the top executive what is happening in the business and how he can make adjustments to meet customer demand. Otherwise, the top executive goes out of business.

The great economist and philosopher Ludwig von Mises, in his classic *Bureaucracy*, eloquently stated what makes the modern business corporation unique:

> The elaborate methods of modern bookkeeping, accounting, and business statistics provide the entrepreneur with a faithful image of all his operations. He is in a position to learn how successful or unsuccessful every one of his transactions was. With the aid of these statements he can check the activities of all the departments of his concern, no matter how large it may be. There is, to be sure, some amount of discretion in determining the distribution of overhead costs. But apart from this, the figures provide a faithful reflection of all that is going on in every branch or department. The books and the balance sheets are the conscience of business. They are also the businessman's compass.... By means of this ... the businessman can at any time survey the general whole without needing to perplex himself with the details.

This is precisely what the government executive cannot do. He has neither "conscience" nor compass that tells him "all that is going on," so he cannot delegate without being "perplexed." Yes, there are thousands of budget figures, but even the budget directors in their candid moments (see, for instance, David Stockman's book, *The Triumph of Politics*) admit they don't mean much.

But the government is *there*, and it needs to be managed. So, the public executive must proceed to manage without bottom lines and reliable data. So, without reliable fiscal management tools, he is forced to rely primarily on personnel management.

Jimmy Carter ran for president saying the American bureaucracy had become rigid and irresponsible, unable to achieve its goals, and needed to be made more responsible. When elected president, Carter instructed my predecessor, Dr. Alan K. Campbell, to take this theme and make it into law, which he did by skillfully working the Civil Service Reform Act (CSRA) through Congress in 1978. The CSRA was the great accomplishment of the Carter administration, a monumental step forward in improving the operations of government.

The Carter administration deserves the thanks of all Americans for this singular achievement. But let me illustrate why Jimmy Carter was not successful with his own management reforms. Reflecting in his memoirs, *Taking Care of the Law*, on his tenure as Carter's attorney general and on the backhanded bureaucratic techniques used to frustrate his efforts at reform, Griffin Bell wrote:

> A major contribution to this sad state of government is the absence of fear—fear of the discipline that one would expect to stop the use of the techniques. There is no discipline in the bureaucracy comparable to that in the private sector if these techniques were attempted there. To be sure, some burying and playing-it-safe goes on in the corporate world, but it is not accepted nor as widespread. The harm done to the Republic by a bureaucracy out of control—a major theme of this book—has led to a state of government that is at the center of our current problems. As the bureaucracy flourishes and expands with no real attempt being

made to measure its work product—to correlate people hired
with work done—it causes government spending to rise, and
thus contributes to the scourge of inflation.

Although Judge Bell understood the problem facing him,
one finds it remarkable that he does not even mention the
CSRA in his book. President Carter and Director Campbell
began to reform government management, but the leadership of Carter's administration was not aware that those
two were creating the tools that would allow it to control
the bureaucracy. Then, too, time simply ran out.

President Reagan knew what to do when his opportunity
knocked. His very first act as president, even before he left
the Capitol after his inauguration, was to put a total freeze
on federal employment. Before he took office, he had
appointed me head of the transition team for all of the government's personnel agencies, and I had briefed his incom-
ing cabinet members and other political leaders on the new
political theory of administration embodied in the CSRA
and the tools it made available to us. From the very beginning I explained the improvements the act had given us,
how we could use them successfully, and how we must set
as our top management priority the full implementation of
CSRA by its legal target date of October 1, 1981.

Immediately the Reagan administration was subjected
to pressure from the civil-service unions, executive and
managerial associations, and their allies in Congress to
delay implementation. I was convinced that delay was a
tactic to frustrate reform. Therefore, I dramatized the need
for implementation by October 1. Thus began what came
to be called my "combative" tactics. Without them, we never
would have implemented CSRA, much less gained control of
the government. For, unless an idea is public in Washington,
it cannot remain on the agenda of the very busy people
who make and influence decisions.

And making civil service issues sexy demanded dramatic
action, indeed. President Carter, after staying up much of the
night before the signing ceremony to read his new CSRA,
told my predecessor the next morning, "This really is boring

stuff, isn't it?" But, with dramatic actions, it was possible to keep the idea of bureaucracy reform in public circulation and to keep up the pressure.

By October 1, 1981, the Reagan administration had implemented the new performance appraisal system by delivering performance standards and elements of individual jobs to 1.7 million federal employees, and we also implemented the bonus-for-performance and merit-pay-for-performance systems for over a hundred thousand executives and managers. This was a huge management achievement, without which the administration never could have implemented President Reagan's policies as well as they were.

I had been chosen for the civil service job because of my theoretical background as a political science professor and my political organizing skills as a campaign consultant. John P. Sears, then campaign manager, had early on asked me to chart for the transition how the new administration should be organized under *political* management principles. But what a difference a state makes! When Reagan lost the Iowa caucuses during Sears' leadership of the 1980 nomination process, Sears was eventually removed from leadership, and my role shifted to planning and state operations. During this critical period, the new leadership reverted to the traditional Republican view of administration by staffing according to the criteria of private sector skills, disregarding Mises' distinction between private and public sector management.

But by no means did all the leaders of the new administration hold these views. Although the initial appointments to the administration were based more upon the possession of private sector skills, the Kitchen Cabinet (a collection of long-time close Reagan associates) and the political division of the campaign remained convinced of the necessity of staffing the administration with those possessing political skills.

My nomination to be director of the Office of Personnel Management (the primary civil service agency) became the battleground for the internal warfare over the two competing viewpoints. After the first round of appointments had been given to corporate types, the Kitchen Cabinet and the political leadership—especially Joseph Coors, William Wilson, Jaquelin Hume, Lyn Nofziger, William Timmons, and all of the regional political directors from the campaign—drew the line at the appointment of the director of OPM. I had been tentatively selected by the Sears plan to be its incumbent, but with Sears gone my appointment was vigorously resisted by those with the competing perspective. At one point, a corporate "headhunter" had been placed at the top of the list for appointment at OPM.

The columnist Robert Novak—helped by leaks from the Reagan political directors, which leaks were begun by Kenneth Klinge—made the issue of my employment the litmus of whether or not long-term "Reaganauts" would be put in positions of authority in the Reagan administration. When his column was published in the *Washington Post*, the issue was joined and the faction representing the political viewpoint carried the day for my nomination.

I have never been able to understand why the simple truth that politics is political is so little understood in American government. This is true even though as a political scientist I was aware that academic interest in the administration of government had largely fallen to intellectuals in the field of "public administration." From the time of its organization under the leadership of Woodrow Wilson, this discipline held that "administration" should have exclusive sway over government after the "political" campaign. Public administration theorists argued that administrators could be deemed neutral on policy because members of the bureaucracy could serve any policy viewpoint, hence policy implementation could be safely left in the hands of career civil servants.

My field of political science generally was not so naive. It recognized that policy cannot be isolated from administration, and that the political leadership needs to be actively involved in the details of administration or it will lose control of the political agenda for which the election campaign was waged.

For some reason, Democrats realize this fact and tend to follow the political scientists. Republicans, however, follow the public administrationists—perhaps because their numbers include so many corporate business administrators. But big business is different from government. There can be "neutral" business administrators because top executives can keep control of policy through the bottom line while still delegating lower-level assignments. Government differs in that top management cannot delegate *without also delegating policy control over the political agenda*. I made it part of my task to make the Republicans as wise as the Democrats.

The political heart of administration is people. And the way these people think about how public organizations are managed is important for good government. It is not that all tenets of public administration are invalid. The way a policy is carried out has neutral, technical elements. But these are clearly subordinate to the central idea of a theory of political administration: the political leadership must set a political agenda *and* ensure that it is carried out.

One of my first objectives as director of the Office of Personnel Management was supporting those in the White House who wanted to select political appointees for political positions, and ensuring that sufficient numbers of political positions (which were under my control) would be available. I also set the policy for what I considered the necessary corollary: career positions should be reserved for members of the career civil service. It is not necessary to subvert the career bureaucracy with hidden political appointees. Career executives should have their protected sphere of authority consistent with the tenets of public administration, as long as there are enough political appointees with the necessary authority spread throughout the bureaucratic structure to provide the leadership.

The president himself set the course for fulfilling this plan. A few months after taking office, he instructed his White House Office of Presidential Personnel that political and philosophical loyalty should be primary considerations in making appointments. Of course, individuals would also have to possess the necessary technical skills.

Unfortunately, by then the personnel for the White House, the cabinet, and some of the subcabinet had been selected. If this policy had been clearly enunciated earlier, many problems created by appointees lacking loyalty to the president or necessary political skills or philosophical grounding would have been avoided. In any event, the groundwork had been laid, even if belatedly, for an effective political administration.

My first official speech, given to the American Society for Public Administration in March 1981, made clear our new approach to government administration. The subsequent publication of this speech supposedly generated the largest number of requests for copies ever received by the *Public Administration Times*. However, understanding of the new policy remained limited to the public administration establishment—both in the academy and in the bureaucracy—and to those parts of the administration I had targeted for speeches, briefings, and symposia on how political appointees should govern. Jim Crawford, columnist for the federal employee weekly newspaper publication, the *Federal Times*, caught on about a year after I took office. The very perceptive columnist for the *Washington Times*, Tom Diaz, soon recognized I was acting under what he called "Theory Three."

Theory One was that I was a rigid ideologue obliviously pursuing my goals regardless of the consequences. Theory Two was that I dramatized my political agenda and sought confrontation with Congress and the media just for the hell of it. Theory Three was that I was implementing a new theory of administration aimed at getting control of government: raising management issues to public attention by taking dramatic public stands to ensure that employee compensation, work practices, and personnel issues that had been ignored in the past would have the public support to be reformed administratively where possible, and before Congress where necessary.

There *was* a carefully conceived personnel program based upon a new political theory of administration. The program was crafted during the transition to ensure that President Reagan could actually govern, and carry out his "Reagan revolution." Call it Operation Swift Sword. It was based on sound theory and was a pretty good program.

And it worked.

The essence of the plan was for OPM to organize the political leadership in the agencies so that it would have the power, skill, and moral support to manage the agencies. The CSRA carved the executive functions out of the old Civil Service Commission to create an Office of Personnel Management as a tool for presidential control of the bureaucracy, and placed the judicial functions in a Merit Systems Protection Board. Previously, the CSC combined within itself both the mission of managing the civil service to achieve a president's goals and adjudicating employee complaints of abuse as if it were a neutral arbiter. Freed of most of the burdens of arbitral neutrality, the director of OPM could now use his powerful central office, with authority over all civilians in every government agency, to provide strong leadership of the bureaucracy for the president.

As director of OPM, I drew the core political managers in the agencies into the creation and execution of a coordinated plan to provide the leadership necessary to carry out the president's and cabinet's policy agenda. We used the new management tools of the CSRA with these results: work-appraisal and reward practices were made more efficient means for management direction; budget pressures were employed to reduce bloated and counterproductive employee benefits and wasteful spending generally; and, nondefense government employment levels were targeted for reduction—this being viewed as the chief way of permanently reducing the obesity of government.

Basically, this plan worked. The president provided the leadership and his management team more or less carried it out. We were successful beyond my wildest dreams in making the bureaucracy more responsible and in achieving

budget and personnel savings. But, as shown below, difficulties lay along the way, some even engendered by those who
were supposed to be helping.

I

The White House

2

Ronald Reagan and the Smart Guys

Ronald Reagan was a great president, in spite of his staff, because he inspired the American people so successfully that his values of "God, family, freedom, neighborhood, work" set a new tone for the nation. My book *The Political Culture of the United States* had demonstrated what Reagan knew, that these values have been deeply held by most Americans since the nation's founding. But because our cultural elite found them not trendy, few politicians dared express them publicly. I first suggested to then-Governor Reagan that he use that phrase for advertising during the Illinois primary in 1980. The people rewarded Ronald Reagan for the way he embodied those values by twice electing him with extraordinary majorities.

The President Meant What the
White House Staff Said

The president's White House staff was very "smart." Some staffers did what the president wanted because they respected him and his authority. But most were smart guys who "knew" that words were to be used only to manipulate, that rhetoric was simply hyperbole, and that ideas were not supposed to have political consequences. Ideas were symbols with which to manipulate the media, the organized interest groups in Washington, the Congress, and the public. The Old Man's job was to give them the words, and the smart guys' job was to govern.

The smartest guy among Reagan's close advisers was Michael K. Deaver. Deaver had been a long-time associate of Governor Reagan. He specialized in public relations. He knew Reagan intimately. And he knew how to present him very effectively. After Reagan left the governorship, Deaver formed a public relations firm to market Ronald Reagan for the presidency and contributed greatly to Reagan's successful campaign. Of course, Ronald Reagan was no slouch in this business himself, having spent much of his life as an actor. Reagan was indeed a master.

Deaver was also more than a good publicist. He had developed a very close personal relationship with Ronald Reagan and an even closer one with Nancy Reagan, who had great influence with her husband. When I was on the Reagan national staff in 1976, we called Deaver "Sonny," indicating he was a "son" to the Reagans. Just before John Sears removed Deaver from the campaign leadership in 1980, I warned Sears that he would pay dearly for his obsession to remove those close to Reagan, especially Deaver. And he did. No one could win an argument in the long run against Mike Deaver, with the Reagans. Deaver was a most effective inside player.

Edwin Meese III was also a close associate of Ronald Reagan. When he was named the head of the transition after the 1980 election, he assumed he would be chief of staff in the White House. He did not fully understand Deaver. Capitalizing upon Meese's reputation in the campaign for putting memoranda in his briefcase and not taking action upon them, Deaver persuaded the president of the need for a more efficient person to be chief of staff.

Enter James Baker III. Baker was a wealthy establishment Republican who had been called in by President Gerald Ford to stem the Reagan reach for the presidency in 1976. In 1980 Baker was campaign manager for the main candidate opposing Ronald Reagan for the nomination, George Bush. But, after the convention, Baker helped prepare Ronald Reagan for the debates with Jimmy Carter. Baker had a reputation for efficiency, but because of his long association with establishment Republicans like Ford and Bush, Baker had earned the enmity of the conservatives who had nominated Ronald Reagan.

Baker, therefore, had the essential qualities Deaver needed. Baker had a reputation for efficiency, but not too great a one (Bush and Ford lost, after all), and he could never be trusted by the conservatives who were Ronald Reagan's base of power. Therefore, Baker's tenure as chief of staff would always be threatened by those on the right, who would never allow him fully to consolidate his power. This opened the door for Deaver, who would become deputy chief of staff, to keep control. Deaver sold the proposal to the president that Meese was not efficient enough to be chief of staff but would make an excellent chief policy adviser as counselor to the president. He raised the name of Baker as chief and himself as deputy. Since Meese would be given a major role in his strongest area of policy, the president approved the proposal.

Meese never knew what hit him. The arrangement was presented to him as a done deal. A troika was set up in the White House with Baker, Deaver, and Meese the major powers under the president. But the power relationships were unequal. Meese would not use what he considered underhanded strategies, like using the media to achieve inside goals. Baker was hobbled by his outsider status.

Deaver thus became the most powerful of the three in the White House.

A former White House chief of staff, Alexander M. Haig, Jr., has stated that three major powers are exercised in the White House: control over the flow of paper, control over the president's schedule, and control over communication to the media. To assess the relative power Deaver enjoyed, one must recognize that Deaver possessed two of the three powers: he controlled the president's schedule and relations with the media.

As for the flow of paper, none of the troika was especially interested in it. All three were known for their "clean desks." It was for this reason that Richard Darman, deputy to Baker, and Craig L. Fuller, cabinet secretary and deputy to Meese, became important in the White House. Darman, especially, was an expert on paper flow. Even here, however, Deaver had something special. Fuller had been an assistant at Deaver's public relations firm, and a close relationship also existed between Fuller and Darman. Deaver, therefore, had eyes in the offices both of the chief of staff and of the counselor.

Major power over two centers and intelligence from the third ensconced Deaver in the preeminent position. But Deaver was not satisfied with his formal power, or with the base of his power—his warm friendship with the Reagans. Deaver shrewdly understood that he could use the media to exercise control of the White House and the whole executive branch outside. Baker was later to master this art, but his base was too weak at the beginning. Although Deaver was basically uninterested in policymaking, he was fiercely interested in protecting the president. To the extent that policy could hurt the president, Deaver became interested in it and in the need to manipulate it in a direction favorable to the president. As for protecting the president, Deaver trusted no one else's judgment—including the president's.

Whenever the president made what Deaver considered a blooper, the deputy chief of staff simply gave nonattributed corrections to the press—personally, through

Baker, through communications head David R. Gergen, or through others. Deaver and Company were the really "smart" ones, the experts who were to protect the Old Man even from himself.

To ensure that they could use the media to set policy by correcting the president, the smarties had to ensure media access to White House policymaking. Otherwise the media would not play the game. The smart guys perfected the "leak" to achieve their policy goals. But their policy had little substance, even in their own minds. Policy simply consisted of a means by which to present the president in the image that they believed made him most effective: placing the president on the side of the issue that the media, Congress, and the bureaucracy deemed most "reasonable."

Since the president was not willing to subject his agenda to media or congressional veto, he often disagreed with his staff in his public statements. *He* was interested in policy! Yet, the staff "corrected" him whenever the president spoke his mind. Since the media "knew" the staff was in charge, the press began to report that "the president meant what the staff said."

Who's in Charge?

Secretary of State Haig had been vice chief of staff of the army, NATO commander, chief of staff of the White House, and secretary of state in the Reagan administration. In his book *Caveat*, Haig explained how the Reagan White House dealt with its cabinet from the combined perspective of his earlier experiences.

From the very beginning Haig found the White House mysterious. Nominally, Meese was in charge of policy and he had a logical mind and was capable of keen insights. But Haig thought him limited by his lack of detailed knowledge of how government really worked. Moreover, Meese clearly was not in charge. Baker seemed to have more influence, but he was "elusive." Haig did not trust Baker; Baker never directly said yes or no.

The former military man found all of this confusing:

> To me, the White House was as mysterious as a ghost
> ship; you heard the creak of the rigging and groan of the
> timbers and sometimes even glimpsed the crew on deck. But
> which of the crew had the helm? Was it Meese, or Baker, or
> was it someone else? It was impossible to know for sure.

When something was heard, "no one knew if what they
were saying was the president's policy." But normally they
didn't speak directly to anyone. "If I had difficulty in wrench-
ing opinion from the White House staff when I spoke to them
in person," Haig recalled, "its members conversed with
remarkable fluency through the press." The *Washington Post*
and the *New York Times* became the conduits of counsel to
the secretary of state from the White House staff. "High White
House sources" began to comment that Haig was ambitious
for the presidency himself and said that he was earning the
title "Commander in Chief of the World." The prestige press
began to report numerous confidential discussions and policy meetings. When Haig confronted Meese or Baker, each
would respond that it was "just newspaper talk, Al."

Haig basically had unraveled the mystery. It *was* "someone else." But it did not seem possible to the military man
that "someone" was a deputy. In fact, Deaver *was* the White
House and he used it to defeat the secretary of state, as he
had Sears and Meese and many others, because he thought
Haig was a threat to the president's image. And he used
the leak to control the other agencies of government just
as effectively.

President Reagan's mode of leadership was to give the
basic policy direction and to trust the person responsible
in the agency, like Haig, to carry out his policy. This was a
marvelous method so long as agency heads understood and
were able to carry out the policy, and were at least ignored
by the White House staff. As long as the agency head had no
trouble with the staff, wisdom consisted in not trying to
communicate with the ghost ship, but simply carrying out
what he knew the president wanted.

If the media paid no attention, the responsible official was on easy street. If they did, watch out. Or, if he crossed the smart guys, they would get him media attention in a most unpleasant manner. Either way, once the media criticized an agency head, Deaver and Company really became a problem. "Bad press" became a criterion of how well he was doing. If it got too bad, as it did for Haig, he had to resign. To say the least, this did not encourage risk-taking among agency heads.

The Report Card

Today, few forces in American politics are more powerful than the mass media. The earliest analysts of American politics, like Alexis de Tocqueville, knew the press would necessarily play a central role in a democracy like the United States. Such insight was developed further by analysts like Lord Bryce, as the media built a corporate base at the turn of the century. By the 1960s, V.O. Key, Jr., could identify the media as one of the most important political forces in the United States. For, as he noted, politicians are not unaffected by how they are portrayed in the media.

In his *The News at Any Cost*, author Tom Goldstein gave due recognition to Time-Life's Henry Luce for his role in promoting Dwight D. Eisenhower to the presidency. Likewise, Philip Graham of the *Washington Post* was given partial credit for the election of John F. Kennedy and full credit for bringing Lyndon Johnson and Kennedy together on the 1960 ticket, thereby making Kennedy acceptable to the South. Ben Bradlee, now executive editor of the *Post* and then with *Newsweek*, played the role of making the Kennedy administration appear successful; beholding the administration through the rose-colored glasses of his personal friendship with Jack Kennedy, he pictured it as a Camelot.

The media role in the Vietnam War helped persuade Johnson not to run for reelection in 1968. And with Watergate, the media increased their power by accomplishing the most powerful political act—regicide. In bringing down

Richard M. Nixon and his assistants, the *Washington Post* sent this message to politicians: crossing the press could imperil their political existence, and threaten jail.

Watergate also marked the arrival of a "new journalism," a much tougher one. Goldstein told of a television film crew that manned its cameras while an unemployed roofer set himself on fire in March 1983, instead of trying to save him. Even though reporters in World War II accepted censorship and even saluted those who outranked them, and the *New York Times* censored itself to protect the Bay of Pigs invasion of Cuba, following Watergate it became routine to publish military secrets. At one point the government had to go to court to prevent a publication from printing an article on how to make an atomic bomb.

Ambush interviews—in which it is impossible, Goldstein noted, for a normal human being not to look guilty—became the way to win awards in television journalism, and the hidden microphone became so essential that its use became normal for political television. As an ABC "20/20" executive opined, on the new rules for twentieth-century journalists, "Ethics to me is a lot of crap." The only thing that counts, whatever the cost to those covered by the media, is an "exciting story." Ethics, honesty, patriotism, loyalty, friendship, and even a human life count for nothing in the brutal game of creating "the story" and getting the glory.

This was the prevailing media environment when Deaver and Company and the Reagan administration entered office in 1980. Any prudent administration would have had to devise a strategy to deal with this new kind of news media. But the government was not powerless in this game. Attorney General Robert F. Kennedy had previously perfected the executive branch leak to indict the head of the Teamsters Union. He prejudiced public opinion by persuading *Life* to run an article that painted a very unfavorable portrait of his target.

Likewise, political leaders could develop friendships with powerful media players to advance careers and policy. The repeated and unusually favorable coverage of the U.S. court of appeals judge Irving R. Kaufmann by the *New York Times* during the 1970s, reported by Tom Goldstein, showed that personal ambition and policy goals could be advanced jointly by clever politicians, even if they wore judicial robes.

The essentials of Deaver's strategy had been known earlier, but he was extremely successful in implementing and refining them so as to maneuver the media into putting the president in a favorable light. There was a cost, however. The Deaver technique forced him to rely upon the media to determine the success of his president and his administration. David Gergen coined the felicitous phrase "report card" to express this dependence. Gergen had said that the White House turned to the television news each night for its report card on how well the administration had done that day.

Of course, this let the media know they had the power to influence the Reagan agenda. Whatever the media chose to criticize, the Deaver White House would be forced to modify—sometimes on the margin, but often basic policy itself because the journalists many times were too clever to be appeased with a wholly symbolic action.

In return for getting this policy role in the Reagan administration, the media were more than pleased to help Deaver and Company. They allowed Deaver to use their communications channels to discipline administration appointees, to manipulate occasionally the press itself on symbolic matters, and even to achieve coverage that could aid the president electorally.

Significant as these gains were for the administration, policymaking became chaotic. Lower-level officials in the White House started playing the game—even preliminary policy documents were leaked—and those in the agencies responsible for policymaking and execution paid the political cost. As awareness of this White House operating procedure started seeping into the agencies, only the boldest of the Reagan administration appointees would do their policy job and take the media heat.

The Great Communicator

Ronald Reagan was able to transcend the smart guys' system when it counted. He was able to do so because he possessed a remarkable strength of character and could so appeal to the people as to inspire them to support him. He was not afraid of the press or of expressing himself when it was necessary to lead. He didn't fear "blunders" because he knew he could communicate the essence, even if the details were not precise.

Reagan could confuse the words but still get the music right, and that is what counts for the typical citizen. The smart guys did not understand how essence could be communicated without bureaucratic mumbo jumbo, numbers, and charts. But Ronald Reagan did. They eventually called him the Great Communicator, but puzzled over how he did it.

The smart guys could not understand how a people who are basically driven by self-interest can also have an altruistic side. They had not read the founders of the American Republic—as Ronald Reagan had—who posited that people have both selfish and virtuous sides, and that it is possible to motivate the good side. The smart guys read nothing but the newspapers, and then only in the daily clip summary. They thought the president not smart and often whispered snide comments and passed sarcastic notes, sometimes even openly at cabinet meetings (in particular, David Stockman and Darman). Yet the smart guys ended up being regarded as trivial, focusing on image and nuance, whereas the president focused on substance and spoke to the people's deeply held values.

Who was successful and by what measure? President Reagan's stated that criterion in his inaugural address, saying that his administration "was not cutting government spending just to save money, but to return power to states, communities, and citizens." Saving money and reinvigorating the economy were short-term goals. The long-term goal was "curbing the size and influence of the federal establishment" and increasing the freedom of the people.

Although the president fell short of achieving all that he sought, it will be shown that he was extremely successful in his essential goal of curbing the size and influence of the federal establishment, and energizing the private sector and local communities. He did it through moral leadership, and despite a White House full of smart guys.

3

Implementing the Mandate

Putting out Brush Fires

Perhaps God wanted to remind us that He is responsible for all good things, for the relative success of President Reagan's revolution could hardly be called well planned. The organizational structure of the Reagan White House generally followed the structure inherited from Jimmy Carter. The White House Office was utilized substantially as it had evolved from its formal beginnings in the late 1930s, as the central organizing institution for the presidency.

And the Office of Management and Budget (OMB) was continued as it had evolved from the Budget and Accounting Act of 1921. It was accepted without debate that the White House Office would set the central policy for the executive branch and that OMB would be used to implement it. To see that all was done lawfully, a myriad of legal offices would review everything. That was how it "always" had been done, right down to Jimmy Carter.

The purpose of the structure of centralized White House staff offices created in 1921—collectively called the "presidency"—was to provide for presidential leadership. In his *Congressional Government*, Woodrow Wilson asserted that Congress was fragmented and reactive to pressures rather than organized as a power for positive leadership as was the British Parliament. The presidency, Wilson and his heirs felt, therefore needed to be a more centralized and bureaucratized force for rational policy leadership and professional coordination, so as to overcome congressional parochialism. But it didn't quite work that way.

President Reagan personally, not the "presidency," forced his economic recovery program through Congress the first year. Thereafter, the Reagan White House Office generally reacted to events, instead of advancing a White House plan as the Wilsonian theory would have it. Craig Fuller, cabinet secretary, explained to me once how the daily agenda was set for the White House senior staff meetings. "We divide up the press stories among the senior staff each morning and use these to assign responsibilities to the staff. I then follow up to see that the assigned individual carries out his responsibility. If necessary, the matter might be referred to Baker, Deaver, or Meese. This is how we operate each day."

The focus of attention in the White House was each day's newspaper headlines. The phrase "putting out brush fires" dominated White House thinking and action. Each day began a new decisionmaking environment unless a story carried over from the previous day. The goal was to eradicate a story from the media's attention, upon doing which the problem was deemed "solved." Then "the world" was begun again the next day.

Before meeting each morning, Edwin Meese, James Baker, and Michael Deaver read the news summaries and then prepared the White House agenda for the day. Deaver, especially, focused on news items that adversely affected the president personally and first moved to solve them. If a story referred to the president, the goal was to direct it toward someone else if it could not be superseded by another story to deflect attention. As long as the media got a new scalp, it mattered little to Deaver and Company whose it was. If the focus of the story was upon a cabinet or agency official, a second-level official like Fuller would be assigned to put out the fire, and he would assign the task to a subordinate. Usually, the easiest way for the White House to get the media off the story was for the staff to tell the agency official to back down on policy.

The lack of leadership from the White House Office and the reactive nature of policy there were just as apparent in the decisionmaking process. White House decision memoranda were given their structure by Edwin L. Harper, deputy director of OMB and later assistant to the president for domestic policy. His method was based upon a memorandum structure he had used in the Nixon White House. Naturally, it had background, analysis, and recommendation sections. Its unique aspect was its justification section, which was called "the action-forcing event." The title is revealing. To arrive at a decision, some event had to force the decision, showing not only the reactive nature of White House decisionmaking, but also the major problem with centralized decisionmaking itself: it becomes overwhelmed.

The Reagan White House took on too much, and decisionmaking became slow, inefficient, and painful, especially when aggressive action was called for. Harper correctly saw that in this environment it was necessary to have something to force a decision. But the "something" chosen was an outside event, rarely a White House initiative.

The Troika

The innovative aspect of the Reagan White House structure in the first term was the creation of a troika consisting of White House Chief of Staff Baker, Deputy Chief of Staff Deaver, and Counselor Meese. This troika was very different from the conventional White House organization, which forced all aides under one hierarchy headed by a single, powerful chief of staff. Richard Nixon had worked through this latter structure, as had Jimmy Carter in his final two years, as did Reagan in his second term. Carter had experimented with a decentralized system with several aides reporting to him in his first term, but he became overwhelmed. A modification of Carter's decentralized system, the troika took into account the reality of the power distribution among the three. Deaver, with control of the schedule and communications, could not be ignored, and Meese, the only one interested in and knowledgeable about policy per se, simply could not be excluded. Each also had longstanding personal relationships with the president.

To ensure close working relationships within the troika, the three met for breakfast at seven-thirty each morning. Here they discussed the day's news events and how they would generally react to them. About eight-thirty, they would convene the senior staff of the White House and make assignments as well as listen to reports from others. The trio might meet with the president later for short visits, all three standing before him, and for longer ones, with the three seated around the president. Papers might be produced for presidential action, or other matters discussed.

During the day the three would attend events with the president. Fuller and Darman did the paperwork. Then Deaver would attend to media and personal appearance events for the president. Baker would begin discussions with the White House staff, giving special attention to his Legislative Strategy Group (LSG) and to Congress. Meese would focus on the policy process, perhaps supervising or attending cabinet council meetings. To assist the members of the troika, Baker had a staff of 300, Deaver 40, and Meese 25.

At the beginning there had been a halfhearted attempt at cabinet government, but the troika quickly consolidated power in the White House. Cabinet discussions would still take place, but the president would rarely make decisions at such meetings. His normal course was to reflect upon the options or recommendations proposed and announce them to the troika when they met the next morning or a few days later. Sometimes decisions would be put off for many days, and sometimes they were not made at all. On issues of great interest to the president, such as firing the striking air traffic controllers and flattening the tax-rate structure, the president would be decisive and fully take charge. On others, especially on complex nonideological issues, Reagan would rely on the troika.

In most cases, the cabinet had little power as a group and became only a discussion forum. Few cabinet participants would speak out on controversial issues, knowing they were not in a decisionmaking forum. Since the president's normal assumption was that his associates were in general agreement, the cabinet meetings reinforced this view. Interior Secretary James Watt was an exception and often spoke up. Others spoke up occasionally, but this only earned them the enmity of the troika.

The major policy decisionmaking body in the White House, the Legislative Strategy Group, was not in the Meese policy chain of command at all. It was headed by Baker, who utilized legislative strategy—normally a process rather than a policy channel—to get leverage over the policy agenda from Meese. It was staffed by Darman, and normally excluded Meese. David Stockman was a central actor in the LSG and indeed achieved his major policy role through this institution. Chief lobbyist Max Friedersdorf and, later, Kenneth Duberstein were important players too, as was David Gergen. Others would be invited to particular meetings. The group easily surpassed in importance the policy cabinet councils established by Meese because the LSG made the final policy agreements with Congress. The basic policy structure might be developed by the cabinet councils, but the final decisions were made by the Legislative Strategy Group.

Since the LSG was the president's highest policy forum and since its source of power was its interaction with the Hill, Congress also received a major role in the central policy-forming process of the Reagan administration. The normal process of the LSG was to factor in congressional opposition before the final policy was developed. This had the effect of the Baker, Stockman, Darman group compromising itself, in Congress's name, before the policy even arrived at the bargaining table with Congress. Sometimes this worked tolerably well when a compromise had been worked out with all congressional leaders well beforehand. Much more often, the White House's already compromised position became the initial offer, which was later further compromised in the House and the Senate bargaining process. The unfortunate result was a policy substantially more diluted than was necessary.

If the White House decisionmaking process was reactive, cumbersome, cautious, and overcompromised, how was the administration initially so successful? The answer was the election of 1980. The first administrative successes and the string of early congressional victories resulted from the momentum created by the type of campaign waged by the president. He had defined clear and precise positions in the campaign for which he could legitimately claim endorsement by his large electoral victory. The president persuasively asserted that the public endorsed his policies to cut taxes and domestic spending, while building up the military and restoring American prestige in foreign affairs. The popular mandate could then be swept into law because it was so clear, everyone felt the country was in serious trouble and the electorate demanded action. However, after the initial agenda had been introduced and partially enacted, other issues came to the forefront. As the election returns receded from memory, the White House Office structure was put to the test.

The structure primarily failed because it could not communicate to its units. The White House became overwhelmed with issues stressed in the media, especially the prestige press in Washington and New York and the television networks. Because the White House Office did not have the legal authority, it could not enforce its opinions. Rather, its only enforcement mechanism was the media. But using the media undermined team loyalty further. As agency loyalty to the White House staff was eroded in response to its tactics with the media, the staff responded with the charge that the agency heads had "gone native," adopting the policy perspectives of their agencies. But the agency heads recognized that they would not be supported by the White House Office, and so they, naturally, retreated to their own bases of power.

I remember a conversation with a cabinet secretary late in our first year, in which Richard S. Schweiker confided to me that the White House Office had undermined him on social security and health care policy for the last time. Although he would work with the president, he would ignore the White House Office. The troika had chased him off the team through their backbiting in the media. He was clever enough not to confront them directly. On those occasions when they did confront him, he got around them because he had the real power.

In the White House, only the president has real power. The "presidency" is his staff, which is either supportive of or off on its own agenda. Certainly, the evidence from the Reagan administration is that to a great extent the latter condition prevailed throughout the White Office, and that the "agenda" mostly consisted in responding to outside events. To extend his power, a president must make his crew cohesive through team-building under a clearly expressed mandate. For most of the first year, the mandate was clear, enthusiasm was high, and appointees worked as a team. But later the ghost ship's crew proved the weakness of Wilson's plan. Instead of the White House Office producing leadership and professionalism, its members were reactive; their lack of teamwork did not allow them to organize and nurture their initial mandate. And soon they became cautious, compromised, and generally ineffective.

Office of Personnel Slot-Filling

The White House Office of Presidential Personnel viewed its job not as team-building, but as filling job slots. Even there, loyalty was not the preeminent qualification, and there was no White House-sponsored training session to build loyalty during the first year. All of OPP's efforts were devoted to reacting to job openings. From the days of the transition, the number of applications swamped the number of personnel assigned to deal with them. The White House did not catch up for three more years.

The Office of Personnel Management did step into the breach, without White House encouragement and, in fact, with some opposition. But I was keenly aware of the need and demanded access to top officials to give them personnel training. I was able to brief the president-elect and his cabinet nominees in Blair House even before the administration began, and afterward. I organized an Executive Personnel Forum, which had regular speakers and a social hour to build a team among a hundred targeted political executives. I met regularly with each major agency's White House personnel liaison officer and the top politically appointed personnel administrator of each agency. One of my special assistants, Mary M. Rose, was given the primary responsibility of coordinating with agency political personnel offices. My head of executive personnel, George Nesterczuk, was in constant contact with the major agency officials to advise them on policy and mechanics, solicit their views, and build a sense of teamwork.

One ally in the Office of Presidential Personnel was Becky Norton Dunlop. She was keenly aware of the need for team-building but was not given sufficient authority fully to implement her ideas within the Office. OPM, therefore, established an informal liaison with Dunlop to accomplish our common purposes. Only her dogged persistence launched the single team-building forum held each year for political appointees by the White House, and her persistence maintained them over the years. With her assistance, OPM drafted and later implemented continuing formal training sessions for political executives. As a result, by the end of the second year, some team-building was at last emerging within the White House.

The leadership of the Office of Presidential Personnel, however, remained too absorbed in the day-to-day activities of making appointments. As congressional opposition intensified over time, the process became more absorbed in appeasing the concerns of Congress over appointments. By the second term, scores of positions were open and many nominations were withdrawn or defeated, many not submitted until the last minute, including my own renomination. Slot-filling was the job, with no coherent plan or purpose. The White House became fully reactive to Congress's assault on the presidential appointment privilege.

One of the jobs I assigned myself was to be counselor to the agency officials whose turn it was to be in the media/White House hotseat. The first was Richard V. Allen, assistant to the president for national security, who was accused of putting a watch he received from a foreign government into a government safe. The charge was so silly I did not take it seriously. But the White House did, so I called him to cheer him up and to let him know he had support. It was not much but it was something. Those to whom I made cheer-up calls eventually represented the Reagan administration honor roll: Brad Reynolds, assistant attorney general for civil rights; Ed Meese, attorney general; Ann Burford, administrator of the Environmental Protection Agency; Edward Curran, deputy director of the Peace Corps; Raymond Donovan, secretary of labor; Robert Rowland of OSHA; James Watt, secretary of the interior; and many others.

None of these people did anything wrong in government, that I can detect, except do their jobs too well. They did what the president and the voters wanted. Yet, with an aggressive opposition party, with opportunistic Republicans in Congress exploiting the process to further their *own* agendas, and with no counterplan in the Office of Presidential Personnel, they were under fire or forced out. By the fifth year, an assistant to the president would concede publicly to a Heritage Foundation briefing that the White House would not even *nominate* a Reagan appointee who had created opposition in Congress— thereby effectively eliminating those who had tried to do their job for the president. By then, the overburdened Office of Presidential Personnel was doing little more than mechanically processing those in the line waiting to fill positions, rather than building a team to fulfill a mandate, while those already in were losing heart or losing jobs.

Office of Increasing Budgets and Regulations

The Office of Management and Budget was supposed to be the principal instrument of the 1921 act for rationalizing the government, to make Congress and the bureaucracy responsive to the president's policy preferences. In most cases, this was supposed to include reducing agency budgets, which were assumed to be inflated. For the Reagan administration's domestic policy, the clear imperative of both policy and management was to reduce spending. My experience, however, was that OMB increased budgets and defended existing spending patterns as much as it cut them. I publicly made this charge long before David Stockman wrote his book, in which he confirmed it. There were, to be sure, many capable and dedicated people at OMB—Stockman, the first year, and Christopher DeMuth and Jim Miller and many others. The problem was the institution itself.

OMB has a large bureaucracy of over one thousand employees. Like most bureaucracies, it defends its turf, and OMB's turf is the existing structure of government. If too much government is cut back, related OMB oversight may be cut back. Even a senior policy adviser in the White House Office, Robert Carlson—who usually disagreed with my opinion of OMB—admitted that in the area of personnel policy he personally observed that OMB resisted changes to the bureaucracy or cutting its perquisites. If government's role was diminished, clearly future opportunities for OMB staff would be restricted, their pay and benefits frozen or cut with those of other employees, and their prestige lessened. Perhaps personnel policy is too self-interested a test of OMB loyalty to presidents, but it may also be the critical one.

I saw the effect of OMB attitudes as we were setting employment reduction policy. Needless to say, the reduction of nondefense personnel was a top priority of President Reagan, not an incidental or limited issue. A very large reduction was made the first year. Then, in late 1981, the president set a goal of reducing 75,000 full-time equivalent employees (FTE) by the end of his first term. The apparent meaning of the president's announcement was that 75,000 slots would be cut, in *addition* to what had been achieved. OMB thought that would be too difficult, so it included the fiscal year (FY) 1981 reductions, which had already been achieved, in the target. The next sleight of hand was in the FY 1983 budget, wherein OMB required only 72,000 of the reductions be cut by specific agencies, hoping the 3,000 difference might somehow materialize. By the FY 1984 budget, 45,000 of the supposed cuts were not assigned as the responsibility of any particular agency.

OPM work force data showed that the targeted reductions would not be achieved even if each agency met its individual targets, and that the president's target would not be met unless OMB changed its personnel accounting method. The issue had to be taken to the counselor to the president and, finally, to the cabinet council on management and administration, where I forced the issue to resolution at last. An acute embarrassment to the administration was prevented because several news organizations, especially *U.S. News & World Report*, had begun to suspect what was happening to the personnel budget figures relative to OPM's actual numbers. More important, the president would not have achieved his major program goal of reducing the size of the domestic bureaucracy, and the cause would have been OMB, the very institution created to give him control over policy.

From my membership on the cabinet council, I also was able to observe OMB's interesting role in the budget process itself. This process became most open to those outside OMB during the agency appeals of OMB budget decisions. These appeals were made to a Budget Review Board composed of Meese, Baker, and Stockman, and ultimately to the president. Adjustments were made by the board on policy grounds without looking at the overall implications for the agency or the larger governmentwide effects. This was left to OMB budget examiners, who added back in the number of people necessary to fulfill the functions added back into the budget. Yet, no discussion was brought back to the board regarding budget decision effects upon the personnel reductions—except later by OPM. That is, the OMB budget process did not fulfill the very function its Wilsonian founders gave in justifying its existence—its presumed ability to assess governmentwide effects.

Over a long period of time career staffers at OMB develop relationships with the agencies they supposedly oversee. Both OMB and agency budget examiners (and congressional staffers too) are the permanent part of the process and will clearly outlast any administration. Often they play a little game out of sight of the political executives in which the career examiner from OMB and the career agency budget official agree to the actual figure, but the budget officer is encouraged to submit a larger one so the OMB adjuster can show his political supervisor that he is doing his job of cutting the agency budget.

Since the political executive at OMB is overextended, supervising many more agencies than he could possibly know in detail, the OMB staff decision rarely is reviewed. The OMB political appointee must assume his staff is loyal, because there is no possible way for him to know all the details. Not surprisingly, the relationship between the career staffers at OMB and those at the agency is closer than their relationship to their changing political bosses at OMB, and also closer than the relationship between the political boss at OMB and his political counterpart in the agency. Because there was little team-building across agencies for political appointees, the close relationships necessary to overcome the friendships among the career staff did not exist.

The close relationships between career officials at OMB and their counterparts at my agency were very apparent from the beginning, even during the transition. My transition team at OPM had to overcome both our own budget staff at OPM and the OMB budget staff to produce our first budget savings. Fortunately for us, the OMB staff was so overwhelmed with the large number of cuts being requested by the president the first year that it had no alternative but to accept the budget demanded by our transition team. Yet OMB fought our budget presentation and used the arguments of our own budget staff against us. Only by threatening to take my case to the president did I succeed in achieving our budget reductions, especially the elimination of the Intergovernmental Personnel Act grants program to state and local governments. Even after the threat, I actually had to appeal to a top political appointee at OMB, Glenn Schlegel, to make this decision stick.

The decision which I can look back upon as having the greatest budget effect of my tenure was my reform of the Federal Employees Health Benefits (FEHB) program. Not only were the policy benefits of the actions I took recognized by the National Capitol Area Health Care Coalition when it granted me a cost-containment award for giving our employees a sounder health system, but I also saved taxpayers $3.6 billion as a result of these actions. Yet, these reforms—acknowledged as beneficial even by a *Washington Post* editorial—were opposed by OMB from the beginning. Not a little pressure was put upon me by the highest OMB officials not to proceed with the reforms, and later to back down from them because of congressional pressure on OMB officials. Because of the media attention generated in the Washington area by my changes, the issue came to the attention of the White House, which also tried to dissuade me. The Deaver group simply wanted to turn off the media attention. But the heaviest pressure came from the OMB staffers, who did not like me messing with their health benefits. If they had succeeded, the Reagan budget would have been $15 billion larger by 1990.

OPM's dominant budget item is the Civil Service Retirement System (CSRS). The President's Private Sector Survey on Cost Control (the Grace commission) said that of all government programs, this one most needed reform. Yet every change I proposed to the CSRS was opposed by OMB. Sometimes, the opposition was merely tactical, following the normal (but perverse) course of compromising away positions within the administration before they arrived at Congress. But all too often attempts were made to scuttle the whole effort. Whatever approach OPM would take to reform employee retirement benefits, OMB would take a contrary one.

The OMB response was not hard to understand. The CSRS is the number one perk to be protected by every career bureaucrat, and those in OMB were leading the charge. An OPM career official who was one of the few exceptions reported to me that the General Accounting Office (GAO) official overseeing OPM stated that he had taken the remarkable step of delaying his own retirement on the pledge to block my efforts at change. OMB's "budget consciousness" is not much different from that of the GAO, Congress's supposedly budget-conscious agency.

During each budget session I worked with my staff at OPM to fashion the most practical reforms to meet budget needs in accord with sound personnel policy. For the first few years, OPM recommended a large number of specific reforms on CSRS, most of them previously suggested by presidential commissions. After the major administration success in placing new federal employees under social security, OPM proposed a more comprehensive reform. No matter whether we took a piecemeal or a comprehensive approach, OPM was criticized for not taking the opposite approach. Each year my proposals were rejected by the OMB staff and the OMB political executive. And each time, I had to appeal to David Stockman personally.

I was not dissuaded in the least by the OMB staff reaction, and I proceeded as if it did not exist. I knew that David Stockman could not confront me before the president as a budget director arguing that I had to spend more. I also was confident that a political appointee like Stockman could approach such an issue with more objectivity than could a career staff member dependent upon a pension, and that because he had more confidence in his own judgment he would not be as dependent upon staff as would the political budget examiner. However, the extent to which he was resigned to the "realities" of the political process, as expressed in his book, has shaken my original confidence.

The OMB staff's protection of its CSRS pension was only a more extreme example of the normal budget process within OMB. The purpose of the budget process was, as several OMB staffers put it to me, to maintain "the presidency." This clearly referred not to the president, Ronald Reagan, but to the institution of the presidency—of which OMB considered itself an integral part. Anything to weaken OMB—its power network with the agencies or its own pensions—should and would be opposed by OMB because it threatened its "presidency." Only strong action by political appointees in the agencies prevented more debilitating action by OMB staff, even though OMB did have a better record in some policy areas during the first term.

Another Office of Management and Budget function is to encourage efficient management practices throughout the government. The OMB Office of Management has a small core staff and a very large number of detailees. All too often, the agencies detail their problem employees, who then try to get even with their agencies from their OMB power base. Our former employees who had been sent to OMB certainly were a problem to OPM in our attempt to make government work more efficiently. OPM's chief contribution to make government more efficient comprised a four-part management initiative: (1) to base pay increases more upon performance; (2) to provide more protection in government layoffs for those with better performance, rather than depend so strongly upon seniority; (3) to make labor-management relations less formalistic/confrontational and more consultative;

and (4) to move overtime pay-setting practices closer to those set by government for the private sector.

These were hardly radical reforms. The Carter administration Civil Service Reform Act (CSRA) had contained a pay-for-performance system for executives and managers, which system had been opposed by OMB then. The section was forced through OMB only when "the president" was given the right to exclude some agencies from its provisions. As soon as the act was passed, OMB was one of the few agencies that petitioned for an exemption to their managers being covered under pay for performance. Naturally, OMB approved the exemption itself in the name of the president. With this history, it was not surprising that OMB opposed extending this concept to the rest of the work force, including itself. How could one ask "the presidency" to be evaluated and paid based upon its performance?

The first tactic by OMB was to use Executive Order 12291, which gives OMB power to review agency regulations and to delay publication of the regulations. This delay was instrumental in giving two Republican congressmen in the Washington area with large federal constituencies— Stan Parris and Frank Wolf— enough time to pressure the White House to wait until after the 1982 elections. Following the election, OMB blocked the rules again so that I had to appeal to the president, through the cabinet council, for approval to publish the rules. After the rules were published for comment, OMB insisted that they be held up again. Finally, just as the regulations were about to become effective, OMB leaked to the chairman of the Senate subcommittee on civil service, Ted Stevens—who also represented a large civil service constituency—that there was opposition within the administration to the regulations.

Stevens pushed a compliant White House Office to compromise and OMB proposed to give him the power to block any one of the four regulations if he would agree that the administration could proceed with the three others. Fortunately, the senator was greedy and insisted on blocking at least two of the four, so I was able to convince the White

House that if we rejected the deal, and so informed OMB, I could negotiate an acceptable compromise. Within four days OMB was neutralized and OPM was able to negotiate a compromise that the federal employees' own paper, the *Federal Times*, said "convinced its foes." Unfortunately, the agreement later became unstuck, partially because OMB continued its opposition, even after the White House intervention, through working with its allies in Congress.

OMB's use of Executive Order 12291 was much more heavy-handed during the Reagan administration than previously. Although I agree with many of the policy results of this intervention, especially for environmental policy, that order is a very blunt instrument. It probably is also illegal. The Administrative Procedures Act and a host of organic statutes give the power to issue regulations to agency heads, not to OMB. Moreover, Executive Order 12291 was debated before the president not as an oversight procedure for the agencies, but as a way to reduce paperwork. I know; I was there.

When that executive order was made even more obstructive of agency prerogatives through Executive Order 12498, OMB maneuvered the proposal through the Cabinet Council on Economic Affairs, whose primary purpose was to consider budgetary, tax, and related matters, rather than through the Cabinet Council on Management and Administration, which had the expertise on administrative issues such as regulations. I argued to OMB that there was an inherent conflict of interest in career staff at OMB reviewing policies proposed by the president's appointees that would have a direct effect on the career civil service. Besides, the Administrative Procedures Act, OPM's own statute, said that the director of OPM, not OMB, had the power to "publish in the *Federal Register*, general notice of any rule or regulation which is proposed." But OPM was not on the economic council and no one heard the debate.

As a result of OMB's power grab, Congress took an interest. The FY 1986 appropriation for the Treasury and certain independent agencies prohibited OMB from changing congressional transcripts of testimony by officials of other federal agencies, and limited OMB review of agricultural marketing orders. Several bills have followed that would take rule-making review away from OMB and return it to Congress. Heavy-handed use of regulatory review by OMB created the threat of a loss of executive power to Congress. For, to an aroused Congress, the alternative to OMB power is not power for the president and his agency heads, but more micromanagement by Congress.

Office of Legal Confusion with Policy

Another inhibitor of executive branch decisionmaking that is sometimes worse than OMB is a relatively recent creation. It is not one organization but several entities working in sequence. These are certain centralized law offices which are little noticed except to those at the top of the government but are given vast authority to effect policy. This thorn in the flesh apparently had its origins in President Nixon's executive order on affirmative action, which created a central legal clearinghouse on civil rights matters in the Department of Justice (DOJ). Today, it has grown to become a powerful triangle: the Office of Legal Counsel at DOJ; the Office of Counsel to the President in the White House; and the General Counsel of OMB.

Originally, Justice's Office of Legal Counsel was established to assist the attorney general in preparing legal opinions requested by the president and the agency heads, but the affirmative action order transformed the Office of Legal Counsel into an office which it could speak upon its own initiative. To this was added the Office of Counsel to the President. This institution gained notoriety from its incumbent during the Nixon administration, John Dean, but it in fact achieved its pinnacle of power when it was used by the White House to purge itself of Watergate. It was especially active under its leader during the Reagan administration, Fred W. Fielding, the former deputy to Dean. The third leg of this centralized legal triad was the Office of General Counsel in OMB, which derived its power from its legal approval of executive orders and its ability to refer regulations from OMB to DOJ.

It had long been known within the bureaucracy and among political appointees that the sure way to kill a proposal was to send it to the agency's office of general counsel. There, various stratagems were used. Lawyers could simply bury it until it became too late to make a decision. A second method was for the agency's office of general counsel to raise a large number of further questions, again providing the necessary delay. For those proposals that really needed a decent burial, a formal legal opinion could be issued saying (or better yet, just suggesting) that it might be legally insufficient. Since every bureaucrat's greatest fear is the word *illegal*, especially after Watergate, that was enough to doom any proposal. This was true no matter how far down in the chain of command the term *illegal* was raised: it could delay or kill any policy proposal. Or the reverse strategy could be used; a nice-sounding legal opinion could help a poor policy by suggesting it was the most appropriate legal one.

The triad perfected the technique of using law to shape policy. No lawyer I dealt with in my four years—and the lawyers were legion—was reluctant to propose policy changes he desired as part of his price for his legal blessing upon the policy document. This not only allowed another large group of cooks into the policymaking kitchen, but also added severe delays even when you gave your payoff promptly. For a decisionmaker in the agency walking a tightrope between the crocodiles in Congress and the sharks in the media, this delay could be fatal.

Inevitably the legal advice from the triad was poor. One of my duties as chief personnel officer was to run the government's charitable drive, the Combined Federal Campaign (CFC). By a series of decisions, political advocacy groups had forced their way into our charitable campaign through the use of litigation and favorable judicial rulings at the district court level. The legal technicalities seized upon by the court to admit these political advocacy groups into the CFC rested upon some loose wording in the executive order that created the campaign. Although the language had been clear for twenty years under five presidents, the lawyers and the courts forced the government to change the wording in the executive order to make perfectly clear all five presidents' intentions. So, we at OPM drafted a new executive order.

From the beginning, the triad insisted that excluding the political advocacy groups from the charity was unconstitutional. The triad argued that this would deny "free speech" to these organizations. Appealing to an earlier Supreme Court decision in the *Schaumburg* case wherein a local government had refused to allow a religious organization to solicit charitable contributions door to door, the triad argued that the Court would force us to admit all tax-exempt organizations into the CFC. From the beginning, I argued that this was a ridiculous extension of the *Schaumburg* interpretation.

I argued on policy grounds that even if it had been declared illegal, we should test it again under a more favorable Court, and I cited the logical reasons why the earlier ruling would not apply. OPM's general counsel, Joseph A. Morris, presented all the legal reasons why the triad's interpretation was insufficient. They would not budge. Finally, the president demanded from me the reason why these left-wing political groups were still in the campaign. His order to have them removed was finally carried out through a new executive order, but it took months. The triad went through its death-by-legal-opinions routine prior to publication of the implementing regulations. Fortunately, the left-wing groups deployed their litigation prematurely against the executive order itself, or else the regulations might never have been issued.

Ultimately, the CFC case was appealed to the Supreme Court. After years of delay the Court said: of course, the government can limit charity drives to charities and exclude political groups, following OPM's reasoning almost identically. Not only did our legal triad delay the necessary work to rebuild the charitable fund and force bad public policy in the meantime, but they proved incompetent lawyers in the bargain.

Indeed, delay and lousy advice rather nicely sum up central decisionmaking in today's "Wilsonianized" federal government.

4

What Worked?

Agency Decentralization

Well, then, what worked for President Reagan? Where he had an active agency head committed to his agenda, his mandate was carried out. Ironically, this was *especially* true where the official later had to resign as a result of political pressures. While these people implemented the policies and made them work, they also took the blame for the hard decisions necessary to achieve them. The Reagan administration won both ways, getting the desired results and diverting the political fallout away from the "Teflon president."

Many top administrators could be cited as ones who successfully implemented the president's program. Some were widely recognized, such as Caspar Weinberger, who managed the buildup at the Department of Defense, and John Lehman secretary at the navy. Others were not as obviously successful. Perhaps the most well known was James Watt, secretary of the interior for the first few years of the Reagan administration. In today's changed political climate, in which the government can promulgate environmental policy alternatives without automatically being smeared as an "enemy of the environment," it is difficult to remember how Jim Watt almost single-handedly revolutionized that policy. Before Watt became secretary in 1981, the extreme factions of the environmental lobby held sway, with demands for absolute purity of air, water, and lands and wildlife to be protected in a nearly prehistoric state, regardless of cost or competing public needs.

Secretary Watt created an environmental policy that brought people into the environmental equation. People do need healthy lands, waters, and wildlife, but they also need jobs, agricultural products, energy, recreation, and water for daily use, Watt argued. With the government owning such a large portion of nation's land—nearly 90 percent in several western states—locking up federal lands in untouchable preserves could not be the government's only goal. Watt set a balanced and commonsense policy for management of natural resources, one that considered both the needs of the environment and the needs of the people for other public goods.

Pursuing this balanced policy was criticized in Washington as extremist. But it was Watt's opponents who demanded the extreme standard of 100 percent in their preservation of the environment. Watt was by no means unsympathetic to the environmental side of the equation. During Watt's three years, the Interior approved or revised nearly three times as many orders for the recovery of endangered plants and wildlife as the previous Department of the Interior. Watt recommended or supported additions to the wilderness systems totaling more than 1.8 million acres. In his three years, he acquired 1.6 million more acres of land to be managed as national parks and wildlife refuges. He established a $1 billion park restoration and improvement program, one of the largest since that of 1956 under President Eisenhower.

But Watt had a new way to manage environmental resources, involving the private sector and local government. Thus, he supported a 25 percent tax credit for private restoration of historic structures. He pledged to the governors of the fifty states that the Department of the Interior would be a good neighbor by including governors in land-use planning and in selling selected land to communities for hospitals, schools, parks, recreation areas, and housing projects. By the end of 1983, more land had gone to the states for school systems than had been conveyed since 1969. Watt also began to sell small tracts of land to ranchers and farmers—land not needed for parks, refuges, or wilderness. Despite criticism that Watt was "selling our national heritage," only 1,342 acres were sold in 1982 and 7,981 acres in 1983.

Second only to returning oil pricing to the market as a means to surmount the "energy crisis," was Watt's policy to allow more energy development. In his three years he leased nearly twice as much onshore oil and gas land as was leased between 1977 and 1980, twice as much offshore land, and three and a half times as much coal land. To hold down the cost of housing, more timber was made available through better management of forest lands. Watt also developed a national water policy that reflected local views of managing water resources, getting governments closer to the people who could also be involved in the process.

Watt not only set policy direction, but also provided strong, hands-on management. By charging fees and increasing revenue from department operations, he was able to *decrease* net budget authority by approximately 14 percent from fiscal year 1981 to FY 1984, even though expenditures grew about 7 percent. He completed action on fifty of the fifty-five rules targeted for republication or revision, to ease government regulations on the economy. Watt reduced the number of payroll systems at the Department of the Interior by 50 percent, with an estimated saving of $2 million per year. He established a cash management system, and saved an estimated $1.2 million in interest-carrying costs. The Interior's full-time permanent work force was decreased about 7 percent, and better controls were established over financial and audit processes. Approximately two million man-hours (or over 19 percent of the amount of time) spent by the public to prepare information for submission to the Department of the Interior were saved by reducing paperwork requirements.

Most important, Jim Watt restored sanity to environmental policy, a remarkable accomplishment. But Watt then carelessly made an insensitive remark, which gave his extremist critics ammunition enough to demand his resignation. Jim Watt paid for his fine public service with his job. Yet he had the satisfaction of knowing he had moved the government's environmental policy from simple-minded preservationism to a balanced conservationist policy responsive to all the needs of all America's citizens. Not a bad legacy.

Despite his legal vindication, Raymond Donovan, Reagan's first secretary of labor, suffered more for his public service than most other public servants have. There is no question in my mind that Donovan would not have been indicted for an alleged payoff supposedly made years before he entered government on such weak evidence were he not in public service. Donovan came from the tough construction environment of New York and New Jersey but no one ever came forward with serious evidence that he was personally connected with the corruption of the largely Democratic public works programs of the New York City region. Yet political opponents in Washington and New York were gunning for him because he initiated real changes in labor policy that raised the ire of powerful union chieftains.

One of government's worst programs was the CETA program to train the unemployed. The costs of this program were excessive, higher than to educate students at Harvard University. An extremely low percentage of those trained ever got productive jobs, most of them performing low-priority jobs for local governments, and often becoming hostage to political machines there. If those jobs ended, usually there were no others, since such job experience little prepared one for the permanent jobs of the private sector. Donovan restructured the program under the leadership of Assistant Secretary Albert Angrisani, who typified numerous tough, intelligent, second-level leaders of the Reagan administration. He was highly skilled in political management and set out to reform CETA. Under the reforms, training was offered for real jobs with future potential, and Private Industry Councils were established to assist in meaningful job training. Under the revised program, not only were the trainees learning real, marketable skills, but taxpayers saved $5 billion.

The big-city machine Democrats and their unions became overwrought that Donovan and Angrisani had changed their patronage-promoting CETA program into a real training program. Moreover, they bristled at the fact that Donovan had reformed the Central States Pension Fund of the Teamsters Union. And not least, they scorned Donovan's recommendation of another of his assistant secretaries, Donald L. Dotson, as head of the National Labor Relations Board, seeing it as a way to redress NLRB's previous bias toward labor bosses. The Department of Labor's own internal union was also at odds with Donovan and his assistant secretaries because they had been able to reduce personnel without any decline in productivity. The union bosses and their political allies pressured, and Donovan was prosecuted. But Donovan, Angrisani, and crew made a difference. They saved taxpayers billions of dollars and gave citizens a more rational labor policy.

For years, the Federal Trade Commission had been known more for its stifling regulation than for its promotion of efficient trade. Too often regulations served more to restrict trade in the interests of existing companies and unions than to protect the public. Coming from an academic background, James Miller thought this was wrong and set as his priority the need to use markets to increase trade and to multiply consumer choice.

Chairman Miller immediately reviewed all regulations to assess their effect upon economic efficiency. Being a trained economist, he was in a position to evaluate the results himself. He set as his primary directive, "first do no harm." With limited resources, he relied upon previous studies to pick and choose those regulations causing the most harm. Miller concluded that vertical mergers and conglomerate mergers, often discouraged by previous government efforts, actually increase competition and lower consumer costs. On the other hand, horizontal mergers were suspect.

In the area of consumer protection, the market was the best resource and harmful activities were targeted. Yet, fraud was a problem and could even justify FTC intervention in certain types of class actions. In general, Miller led the FTC to major changes in trade policy, earning his share of criticism from the established interests in the process. His legacy is that federal trade policy has been fundamentally changed to allow more of a market environment, one that survived his departure through the policies of Daniel Oliver.

Some successful Reagan administrators worked in rather obscure places. The General Services Administration is a little-known yet large and important federal agency. Its mission is to administer the government's property. GSA has two claims to fame. One, before the Reagan administration, was the numerous scandals it had nurtured while managing, leasing, and selling government assets. The other was its ability to complicate every government real-property transaction by making it more expensive and time consuming than necessary. GSA had been headed by every possible type of big-business expert, with little success.

Enter Gerald Carmen, a small businessman from New Hampshire who had managed Ronald Reagan's successful 1980 New Hampshire primary campaign. Those who headed the early Office of Presidential Personnel were not impressed with a small businessman and politician as administrator of such a large operation as GSA. Carmen used his political skills to get the job anyway. Later, Pendleton James, then head of the Office of Presidential Personnel, admitted that opposing Carmen for GSA was his worst personnel error.

Carmen said his job was to turn GSA into the government's "business manager instead of its janitor." But first he had to control the pervasive fraud and corruption. In the decade before he took charge, more than one hundred forty employees and contractors were convicted of bribery and other wrongdoing. The agency had been under steady investigation by the Internal Revenue Service and the Department of Justice for decades. Carmen simply announced he would not tolerate corruption but would prosecute it, and there were no charges of corruption during his tenure. Moreover, government office space was reduced by 22 percent under Carmen by consolidating offices and putting more people into the same space. Deliveries of supplies to other government agencies were reduced from an average of forty-one to seven days. And the average time needed to negotiate leases dropped from 366 to 200 days.

Carmen made a difference. He saved hundreds of millions of dollars and brought more efficient practices to the government. At the same time, he slimmed his own staff and reduced corruption. Indeed, Carmen could not understand why there was not more good management. "All you need is the willpower," he would say. "The president has told us to do the job, and we should be doing it. Government is so poorly run that even the incompetent can save money. Anyone can manage better."

ACTION is an independent federal government agency that was created to encourage volunteer charitable activity. The agency had been headed in the Carter administration by the anti-Vietnam activist Sam Brown. Under Brown, the VISTA program of ACTION was used to fund left-wing political activist organizations. This was not surprising since many of the career personnel at the agency were recruited from the 1960s activist movement.

To manage this political jungle, President Reagan chose Thomas Pauken, not only experienced in politics and government, but also a Vietnam veteran. That background led him to recognize that his first job was to recruit an effective and loyal team. He clearly set forth the duty of the team: to effect President Reagan's goal that ACTION aid true voluntary activities, not political causes. So Pauken began to eliminate government support for political activist organizations and promote true volunteerism. As Pauken said, "I didn't make the mistake of shifting funding from political groups on the left to those on the right. The federal government shouldn't be in the business of funding political organizations of whatever persuasion."

What were the results of Pauken's leadership? ACTION's budget was cut from $160 million to $120 million, a 25 percent decrease. Even with this large decrease, new initiatives supporting true voluntary efforts were established, including the Vietnam Veterans Leadership Program, the White House/ACTION Drug Abuse Education and Prevention Program, and an assistance program to help runaway youth with limited financial resources and sizable volunteer support. All political funding grants were eliminated. And there was a 50 percent reduction in ACTION personnel, from 1,000 to 500 employees.

Asked to explain how he was able to accomplish so much, Pauken characteristically gave the credit to President Reagan. Reagan, he said, had outlined the general policy direction of the VISTA program and stressed the inappropriateness of funding political activities with government money in his public pronouncements over the years. Then the president was wise enough to let the agency head decide how to get the job done— and, I would add, smart enough to appoint Pauken to do it.

How were these five and so many others successful? What did they have in common? Three attributes, as I see it, they shared: a loyalty to Ronald Reagan; a strength of character, which motivated them to do a good job; and political experience. Whatever some of them may or may not have done before or after, while in office they mustered the moral courage to take the tough steps necessary to accomplish what President Reagan wanted. Carmen, Donovan, and Pauken had political campaign experience, and Watt and Miller had been in political interest groups.

Only Carmen and Donovan had any real business experience. Apart from strength of character, their political backgrounds made them especially effective managers in an inherently political environment.

These were the most spectacular successes, but many more examples could be included. For example, almost every domestic agency head cut his or her personnel by 5 percent or more. The leaders—some reluctantly forced to virtue by the president—were Terrel Bell at Education, down 24 percent; Sam Pierce at HUD, down 22 percent; OPM, down 19 percent; and Carmen at GSA and Donovan at Labor, down 15 percent (as measured by standardized work-years). For the smaller agencies, Jim Miller at the FTC cut personnel by 28 percent; Reece Taylor at the Interstate Commerce Commission, by 35 percent; Bob Rowland at the OSHA Review Commission, by 40 percent; and Pauken, the champion, by 50 percent.

These and many others less well known made the Reagan revolution. The domestic welfare state was reduced by cutting budgets and people and by loosening its regulatory grip on the productive forces of the private sector. By the time I left the personnel office, nondefense work-years by the federal government were down 6.8 percent over when we entered office. Total nondefense government employment consisted of 105,484 fewer bureaucrats than in 1980, the greatest decline since just after World War II. The Reagan revolution was successful where it was successful because the president set the goal, chose political appointees committed to his program, and allowed them authority to implement it on their own initiative.

Cabinet Councils

One of the most frustrating aspects of government management is that policy responsibilities are divided among different agencies of the government. Nearly every department has an effect on economic policy, but just the major players must include Treasury, Commerce, Labor, and the

Federal Trade Commission. Defense policy includes at least the offices of the secretaries of defense, army, navy, air force, commerce, and energy. Environmental policy includes, at least, Interior, Environmental Protection Agency, Energy, and Transportation. Indeed, there are few policies that do not affect every agency in one way or another.

In this environment, it is necessary to have a coordinating mechanism. In theory, the cabinet was that instrument. But there is so much overlapping in government that the cabinet itself would be overwhelmed if every agency were represented.

One of the sounder innovations of the Reagan administration was the invention of cabinet councils. These were conceived by Edwin Meese as subcommittees of the cabinet. Each council was chaired by the president, but with very active pro tem chairmen. In most cases, the pro tem was the senior cabinet member—Secretary of the Treasury Donald Regan for economic policy, or Counselor Meese himself for the Cabinet Council on Management and Administration (CCMA). Councils were established for overlapping policies touching economic affairs, the environment, energy, etc.

I can speak best about the CCMA, since OPM was a member. The CCMA was extremely useful to OPM as it gave me opportunity to present new programs to the heads of the other major agencies of government and to receive suggestions from them. Although I was invited to the many cabinet sessions that dealt with personnel or management matters, OPM, like EPA and many others, did not have a permanent place on the cabinet. So the CCMA became an especially useful alternative forum. Moreover, the council served the invaluable function of providing a formal mechanism to resolve agency logjams, especially those caused by OMB. Clearly, OPM's reform to make performance central in personnel decisions, its reforms of the retirement system, and the restructuring of the government's charitable drive could not have happened if CCMA had not provided the means by which OPM could secure presidential support to get around the White House Office or OMB.

My most rewarding moment with President Reagan occurred after I had presented OPM's package of management reforms at a CCMA meeting and received the president's approval. As usual, the president ended the meeting and began walking to the Oval Office at the prodding of his staff. Assuming he had left, I began talking to my director for policy, Patrick Korten, who had assisted in the presentation. After several minutes, I noticed out of the corner of my eye that someone was standing quietly nearby, awaiting the completion of my conversation. To my astonishment, it was the president of the United States, too polite to interrupt. He drew me aside and congratulated me on my proposal. And then he turned his head, gave me a wink, and said, "You keep on top of those bureaucrats, and don't let up."

The cabinet councils were by no means the only coordinating institutions that brought the top officials of the government together to deal with common problems. I also served on the President's Council on Integrity and Efficiency, which coordinated the governmentwide attack on waste, fraud, and abuse in government, and one of my senior assistants served on the President's Council on Management Improvement and another on the General Counsels Committee. Most of these and others were unproductive because representatives were from too low a level and did not necessarily reflect the views of the agency head. Indeed, CCMA itself had a secretariat of lower-level officials and it was routinely overruled by the full CCMA.

OPM organized two high-level intergovernmental personnel management councils. The most useful was the Governmentwide Personnel Policy Group (GPPG), consisting of the assistant secretaries for administration in the major cabinet and subcabinet agencies of government. It also included a personal representative of the agency head, normally the same official who coordinated with the White House Office of Presidential Personnel. For most of the first term, one or more representatives of the Office of Presidential Personnel in the White House attended GPPG meetings. GPPG met roughly once every six weeks, and more often at the beginning. I found it an invaluable means through which to formulate personnel policy decisions and then to communicate them between OPM, the White House, and the agencies. It also was the formal structure through which very important informal contacts between agencies, OPM, and White House political appointees were established. It was an invaluable mechanism through which to set and implement policy in a collegial setting.

The second personnel coordinating council was the Executive Committee of the Inter-Agency Advisory Committee on Personnel. This committee had fallen into inactivity during the previous administration when my predecessor ceased meetings because of its adamant opposition to President Carter's CSRA reforms; this council was composed of top career officials in the government personnel community. From the beginning, it was apparent that the career personnel community would oppose most of the Reagan personnel initiatives. However, I felt it was necessary to try to gain as much acceptance from this part of the bureaucracy as I could. Therefore, I immediately reestablished these meetings with the senior career personnel officers of the agencies, especially those from the larger agencies. We consulted with, and accepted recommendations from, this group as far as it was possible without compromising the essentials of the president's program. Although the group was resistant, some acceptance and mutual understanding were gained. I respected most of the officers and found them true professionals. Yet they were so attached to the status quo!

At bottom, though, the council system worked, within predictable limits. If these councils were relatively successful, why were they later merged into a single domestic council? Undoubtedly, the major reason was to continue Edwin Meese's involvement in governmentwide domestic policy. At this point, Meese had moved from the White House to the cabinet, becoming attorney general. Consolidation of the councils under a single mechanism enabled the president to keep the trusted Meese involved with the same domestic agenda the president had him supervising as counselor. In addition, the councils had always had a confused organizational structure within the White House, partially responsible to the Office of Policy Development and partially to the Office of Cabinet Affairs. To accommodate the personal relationship between the president and Meese and to solve internal White House rivalries, the consolidation may have made sense. Structurally, for the whole government, the cabinet council system was far superior; the consolidated domestic council fell into relative disuse in the second term.

Confronting Congress

Four institutions work to tear apart any president's mandate. To an extent, they come with the territory; they're part of the plan of American government to check and balance each branch. Congress was to balance the executive's tendency toward appropriating too much power. The executive was to provide leadership for what otherwise would be a hopelessly parochial legislature. The judiciary, expected to be the weakest branch, was to appeal to the Constitution to rally the people against executive and legislative abuse by force of reason and legal precedent. The constitutionally unrecognized institutions, the bureaucracy and the media, were expected to be controlled by the three constitutional bodies, by the federal structure, or by the people directly.

This divided constitutional order of power has survived to become the oldest continuous constitutional structure in the world. But it was only President George Washington's personal character that prevented his dominant executive branch from overwhelming the newly created Congress. And Thomas Jefferson's politically united executive and legislative branches did not overwhelm the judiciary only because of Chief Justice John Marshall's nimblefootedness and President Jefferson's restraint.

Likewise, Abraham Lincoln's suspension of the right of habeas corpus and other extreme uses of martial law powers clearly overwhelmed the legislative branch, which took its revenge when Congress came within one vote of impeaching President Lincoln's successor. Franklin D. Roosevelt's powerful presidency was restrained only when, after he tried to pack the Court and rid his party of conservatives, FDR was rebuked by a conservative electoral resurgence in 1938. And in reaction to Richard Nixon's executive excesses of Watergate, Congress had by 1980 enfeebled the presidency, with Jimmy Carter suffering the consequences.

Yet the balancing nature of the American regime allows presidents to reverse declines in their power. As President Reagan began to achieve policy successes, assisted by his winning personality, the institution of the presidency revived. The survey research center at the University of Michigan has charted the trust of the people in their government since the 1950s. Its poll data reveal that trust in the government grew dramatically during the Reagan presidency. Republican control of the Senate, gained in the 1980 election, also changed the atmosphere so that the president could deal more equally with Congress. Even with this, the president could prevail over the parochial power of Congress only on issues of high public awareness. Issues of low popular awareness remained hidden in the bowels of the national legislature and remained under control of Congress's interest-dominated politics.

The House of Representatives, being closer to local special interests, is especially subject to parochial interest-group political pressure. Congressional pressure is not restricted to purely ethical requests, either. OPM was continually asked to make exceptions to what my House overseers publicly called the sacred rules of the civil service. My congressional relations director, Robert E. Moffit, would often come back from Capitol Hill muttering, "What happened to the Civil Service Reform League, which produced civil service reform in the nineteenth century; there surely isn't any constituency for good government today." Every trip to the Hill produced demands for exceptions for constituents.

The founders rather expected this, but they thought that lively debates on the floor of the House would expose local parochialism to general review, which would control excesses. In my area of government management, there was not sufficient public interest to force public debate. Congressmen and their staffs knew how to take appropriate advantage of this, and they knew how to avoid such formalities as floor consideration altogether. For example, the Civil Service Retirement System, one of the largest programs in government, was completely restructured by the House without one single minute of floor discussion. Rather, this multi-billion-dollar bit of legislation to benefit federal employees was added by the Senate to an innocuous House bill to name a post office and never saw the light of day in the body that represents the people.

Given this surreal atmosphere for government management issues in Congress generally, OPM congressional relations often were bizarre. And we had to be tough players in the rough-and-tumble legislative environment where the basic fact of life was that politically active federal employees and retirees lived in every congressional district and were the predominant special-interest voting block in at least twenty. Consider my relations with a House subcommittee chairman, Patricia Schroeder, and a member of my appropriations oversight committee, Steny Hoyer, each having large government employee constituencies. The conservative newspaper *Human Events* recounted my running battles with Schroeder and Hoyer in amusing and instructive detail:

> Office of Personnel Management Director Don Devine is not a very popular fellow with congressional liberals and federal employee unions. In fact, because Devine has spent his two and a half years in office tirelessly calling attention to things like the automatic "merit" pay raises federal workers receive, the pay "comparability" surveys rigged in favor of the federal employee, and the massive, soaring costs of

the civil service health and retirement programs, he's become something of a hate figure to the political left.

The resulting notoriety has made him a target of employee union allies like Representatives Steny Hoyer (D-Md.) and Pat Schroeder (D-Colo.), both of whom sit on the Post Office and Civil Service Committee, which is charged with "oversight" of federal pay and employment practices. Time and time again, these lawmakers have tried to rein in—or simply embarrass—Devine in retaliation for his reform efforts. But on one occasion after another, the OPM chief has turned the tables on his political foes....

Schroeder, for example, released a civil service subcommittee report about OPM's efforts to oust the militantly pro-abortion Planned Parenthood from the federal government's annual charitable fund-raising drive. In mid-September, Devine had announced his finding that Planned Parenthood did not meet the CFC's financial guidelines (a decision that was later overturned by liberal U.S. District Judge Joyce Green). In issuing the report, Schroeder, noting Devine's affiliation with the anti-abortion group LIFE-PAC, slammed Devine's conduct in the case as "outrageous" because he allowed "his personal animosity toward an organization to so heavily influence the performance of his official duties."

A few days later, Devine wrote Schroeder back saying that he had read her report on the campaign "with interest, although I found it unremarkable, since it contains nothing that has not already appeared in the daily press over the last three years. In fact, the only omission is the lack of mention of your own special relationship with Planned Parenthood. Your official biography states that you were legal counsel to Planned Parenthood of Colorado, and thus have a long-standing personal involvement in the affairs of the organization whose interests you now so stoutly defend. It might have been well to note this interest for the benefit of the general public, whose tax money paid for the report."

Devine told Schroeder that she had, however, "performed a valuable service in drawing together, in a single report, all of the many documents which have been produced on this issue over the past several years. It describes, among other things, the way I bent over backward to accord due process to Planned Parenthood, and in general is a handy reference guide which I intend to keep close at hand."

That was not the first time Devine had tangled with the left-leaning Coloradan. Several weeks before, Schroeder, in an attempt to increase pay for State Department bureaucrats, advised the OPM director that OPM employees doing the same work were receiving higher pay. Devine looked into the situation, agreed, and promptly proceeded to downgrade the OPM jobs for future hires.

In a letter to Schroeder, Devine said that while "you now state that the clear purpose of your letter was to 'encourage' me to upgrade the [positions of] retirement claims examiners in the State Department, I could not overlook the clear statement in your October 25 letter that you were disturbed about the classification of OPM's retirement claims examiners or your suggestion that the grade disparity smacked of favoritism for employees of my agency."

"Whatever the intent of your inquiry," he went on, "it served to focus the spotlight on [the] classifications at OPM" that were faulty, and therefore had to be lowered. "The option you now suggest, upgrading properly graded State Department positions to [achieve] equity with improperly classified OPM positions, simply would not be legal."

But Schroeder isn't the only liberal lawmaker who has been stung by Devine. Maryland's Hoyer has himself been repeatedly burned by the OPM director. On October 25, for example, OPM proposed its third set of pay-for-performance regulations this year. Despite the fact that OPM had substantially modified the original proposals in an effort to meet critics halfway, Hoyer—who opposes any real reform of the current system—attached an amendment to a continuing resolution barring OPM from spending money to implement two earlier versions of the reforms.

But Hoyer, apparently hoping that OPM would move to further accommodate his concerns, did not extend the ban to the October 25 regulations. Taking advantage of the opportunity created by Hoyer, Devine moved to implement the October 25 reforms (though the National Treasury Employees' Union later filed suit to block them, and was granted a temporary restraining order pending resolution of the case).

Interestingly, when the liberal Marylander attached his anti-OPM amendment, it included language banning the federal employee health benefits plan from paying for abortions except to save the life of the mother, a limitation Hoyer—an "abortion rights" backer—opposed. Reportedly, he hoped the Senate would remove the abortion curbs, but that never happened. The result was an important victory for the pro-life forces—thanks to Steny Hoyer.

While the abortion lobby was predictably livid over what had happened, Devine issued a statement "commend[ing] Mr. Hoyer for his successful effort in the Congress in behalf of protecting the life of the unborn."

The continuing resolution fiasco was not Hoyer's only fumbled attempt to hamstring Devine. Earlier this year, he asked the General Accounting Office—the investigative arm of Congress—to look into an OPM press release blasting Hoyer and other Democrats for placing "obstacles before the kinds of sensible management reforms that would make government work better," as an example of OPM illegal lobbying. But the GAO cleared OPM of charges that the release violated restrictions on the use of federal funds. Congressional liberals, in short, seem to have met their match in Don Devine.

Well, maybe they hadn't, but they knew I was there. And we had fun making sound policy in the wild world of parochial House of Representatives civil service politics.

On the Upper(s) House

For all its fun and games, the House of Representatives was not as great a barrier to good government administration as was the Senate. Notwithstanding the unruliness of the House subcommittee chairmen with authority over civil service—Don Albosta, Geraldine Ferraro, Mary Rose Oakar, and Patricia Schroeder, and they were a handful—the subcommittees were restrained by House traditions and rules that limited their ability to cause damage. Moreover, the chairman of the House Committee on Post Office and Civil Service, William Ford (D-Mich.), was an intelligent and knowledgeable chairman who exercised some control over his unruly horde. Likewise, the ranking minority leader during my first two years, Edward J. Derwinski (R-Ill.), was of great assistance to him (and me) and, independently, a very capable leader. Even some of the committee Democrats usually acted responsibly, including Congressman Hoyer. And to be frank, there were so many actors in the House that the ability of any single one to cause havoc was limited.

The Senate is a much smaller body. With the breakup of the committee system in the 1960s, a much greater dislocation resulted there than in the House. In the House, committees still exercise some organizational role under the rules, and with the much larger size of the chamber the subcommittees still had enough members to constitute a group. Not so in the Senate, where each legislator became his own subcommittee. The major committees in the Senate, such as finance, were so important and newsworthy they remained real committees with several important senatorial participants to balance each other. In less visible political areas, such as civil service, there was not much interest among senators and one man was Mr. Civil Service.

Senator Service, better known as Ted Stevens, was the Senate subcommittee chairman for personnel management and bureaucracy matters. He was smart, obstinate, and demanding and had his personal faults, but the real problem was the system as, *all* real power over civil service devolved upon him. For one thing, no other senator on the full committee or the subcommittee took any interest whatever in the civil service. The subcommittee chairman ruled by default. As Lord Acton taught long ago: power tends to corrupt and absolute power corrupts absolutely. Senator Service was always able to attach a number of riders regarding civil service late at night on the Senate floor when all were too tired and few cared. Likewise, he was able to bully OMB and the White House by wild shouting and abusive behavior to achieve the rest of his agenda administratively.

Senator Service's greatest stroke was to restructure completely the third-largest entitlement program in government without debate, and with only one dissenting vote. He worked together with the House leaders so they could attach their version of the bill to a meaningless post office–naming bill. And he did. Now, we're talking about a program costing $25 billion per year, with future obligations in the trillions (that's right, not billions). You would be surprised how much can be achieved by one person away from the glare of public scrutiny. Even with trillions of dollars involved!

Senator Service was so used to getting his way that he was dumbfounded that the president had the nerve to renominate me for a second term. He had written the White House and had expressed his opposition beforehand. He had also leaked his opposition to the media. Still, the president persisted. When the chairman didn't get his way, he resolved to bide his time. He appeared to cooperate but delayed the nomination until a means could be found to deny my reconfirmation.

Senator Service was an aggressive and resourceful legislator. Even with the Democratic party in control, he still dominates the civil service agenda, intimidating the executive branch participants and slipping bills and amendments past his colleagues in the Senate, often as the last one on the floor. He has a record to prove his power. Until the Senate system that concentrates power in one or two individuals' hands is changed, similar situations will exist throughout Congress. Several active members on each committee are essential to control the power relationships in a legislature so there will be well-considered legislation and a legislative product that serves the people, not well-organized special interests.

One of Senator Service's "reform" proposals to the government's retirement system would have set up a Federal Retirement Thrift Investment Board with the power to invest as much as $100 billion. The board was planned to consist of two political appointees of the president, the chairman of the Federal Reserve Board, and, incredibly, two representatives of federal employee or union organizations. In addition, an Employee Advisory Committee, composed exclusively of union and employee representatives, would have made recommendations regarding how the board should act.

When I testified against this provision, while director of OPM, a House Democratic staffer saw some interesting possibilities with this board. "We could invest a couple billion dollars in the Grace Company one year, and take it out the next. That would be the end of Peter Grace, and it might teach future heads of government reform commissions not to take their jobs so seriously."

If this seems farfetched, the bill would have made the investment standard to be followed by the board "broad acceptance by participants (that is, federal employees) and the public." To make this clear, the board would be *forced* to consider the views of the Employee Advisory Committee. Not only would such a board intimidate businessmen, because its potential power over their capital would certainly make them reluctant to criticize inefficient government reforms, but who would even bother to tangle with a federal bureaucracy that could determine whether investments or disinvestments could be made in one's own corporation?

Media Policymaking

How could such poor policy become law without public scrutiny? Where were the media to inform the public of such silly, and dangerous, proposals? Except for a small-circulation column I myself wrote after my service at OPM, nothing appeared in the media about this $100 billion investment scheme until long afterward. A basic fact about the media is, they will not present such information unless the issue is dramatized so that it cannot be ignored, and in a manner that the arguments are persuasive. And the sad truth is that government management is short on spectacle.

Awareness of this fact dictated my approach to the media when I was director of OPM. The first major story about this new personnel chief by the *Washington Post* used the word "combative." The *Wall Street Journal* followed using the same term. Utilizing the crowd mentality of the media, I adopted this term for myself, and my self-styled characterization apparently made me interesting enough for the media to cover normally uninteresting civil service issues. I mastered all of the relevant facts and arguments to the point that no one could upend me debating civil service issues. Academics were reluctant to debate me on panels and congressmen were reluctant to be embarrassed by my knowledge, and their lack thereof, at committee hearings. I trained myself to play a role whereby I could inform people about civil service issues forcefully but logically—so I could put pressure on the White House, OMB, Congress, the courts, and even the media.

A great deal of planning of top-level government officials revolves around the media. Washington is government in a fishbowl, and the public official ignores this at his peril. A very large part of our activities in OPM centered around plans to use the media to achieve public policy goals. We became very good at it. We knew the issues and had timing down to a tee.

Often we would plan initiatives for press releases for late Friday to get our message across at a time that was difficult for reporters to "research" and distort the message. One sharp reporter dryly commented after several weeks of such, "Is this your normal Friday night call?"

We put personnel issues and OPM on the map. For better or worse, I became a household word within the Washington beltway. The federal-beat reporter for the *Washington Post* wrote that government employees now put a scare into their children not by threatening the bogeyman, but by saying "Devine will get you." More important, Washington—and to a lesser degree the nation—became aware of the billions of dollars in civil service expenditures. And this allowed us to make reforms.

There was a price to be paid, however. About midway into my term the press began reporting regularly that the "White House" was dissatisfied with me and desired my resignation. Opponents in the White House Office and OMB, primarily among the career staff, kept telling the reporters this was so. I decided to refute dramatically the rumor because I knew the president's position, and the rumor was hurting my effectiveness in dealing with Congress. I issued a message to the press that I would hold a press conference the next day "regarding my future." The next day the vultures gathered, ready to feed upon my carcass. Newspapers had been printing calls for my resignation for over a year. In the charged atmosphere, the Baltimore *Sun* actually ran a story saying I had resigned.

I walked into the emotion-laden room while my staff began unloading thousands of postcards on the table in front of me. David Denholm, president of the Public Service Research Council, had written to his members asking those who wished me to stay as director to write-in their support. I announced to the media folk that eleven thousand public-spirited citizens wanted me to stay and I would. The Federal employees' weekly newspaper, the *Federal Times*, ran a sad banner headline on the front page reading, "I will not quit," accompanied with a picture showing the pile of letters of support.

That was fun. But as Tom Diaz, then a civil service columnist for the *Federal Times*, said at the time, the media sharks would just await any misstep by me. If I put a toe overboard, the sharks would pull me down.

Actually, I thought that we received reasonable treatment from the media, with some conspicuous exceptions of self-serving, especially given the fact that Washington's political elite form a high-class "village" where lobbyists, legislators, revolving-door political appointees, career bureaucratic and legislative staff, and the media are all related or are friends. *Washington Post* editorials on my reforms to make the bureaucracy less like a protective cocoon and more like a risk-taking business were a good example of the exception. But what else could one expect? The person assigned to write those editorials was a former civil servant who told me she had friends in the civil service who needed protecting.

A second example was a *Wall Street Journal* piece. A reporter did a major profile of me but his interview lasted only a minute or two, and he asked only three questions. I could not understand why he was so perfunctory and his subsequent article so biased, until I later learned that his wife was a lobbyist for an organization that had lost on a policy decision I had made.

In a third case, a former student of mine who told me she had deserved a higher grade from me was assigned by the Baltimore *Sun* to cover my actions. Her news stories were not flattering, nor was her weekly column.

The media indeed have their conflicts of interest. In the area of civil service, there were superb reporters like Tom Diaz and Mike Causey of the *Post*. But there were also reporters who had conflicts of interests much greater than those of the government officials they criticized. Nonetheless, the fact of the matter is, one cannot blame poor policy on the media. Political leadership can make changes, even in the face of a biased media. Our four years at OPM proved that with some imagination and courage the story can reach the public, even a story dealing with the sexless area of civil service, and that as a result public policy can be positively affected.

The Courts as Congress

Like the media, the federal courts are to a great degree independent of public control. But they can additionally take away life and liberty. The story of the rise in power of the courts to legislate is well known and will not be repeated here. But I can say how OPM was at least able to avoid being swept aside by judicial lawmaking through forcing decisions to public scrutiny.

I have mentioned the crisis that developed in the government's health care program in 1981. Suffice it to say, we were sued from every direction. Certainly every federal union did its share for the lawyers. Interestingly, though OPM lost a score of cases on several different issues in different federal district courts, it eventually prevailed on all but one at the appeals court level. I believe that the way OPM responded to the district court decisions, at least in part, was the reason the government won.

OPM's approach to the district court decisions was to deal with them forthrightly—claiming the executive's right to manage—contrary to the conventional wisdom among the legal community that to criticize a district court judge's decision publically was to guarantee failure upon appeal. The thinking was that colleagues would support colleagues. I disagreed. When one federal district court judge in the D.C. area brusquely overturned our decision not to support abortions under the health benefits plan without serious legal grounding, I pointed out that his wife sat on the Board of Directors of Planned Parenthood in Washington. When another D.C. district judge issued a decision that was illogical and self-contradictory, I said so. Needless to say, the media were happy to air such "outrageous" truths.

We were outrageous, but we were logical and factual. We showed precisely where the reasoning was poor, or where judicial preferences overrode legal limits and logical bounds. Judges, like anyone else, do not wish to look like fools. Perhaps the fact that we did not recoil into the smothering arms of the lawyers allowed the appeals judges to read the newspapers as well as the briefs. Indeed, I was surprised to note that many court decisions quoted our press releases as much as our legal filings. Whatever, the fact is, OPM won every appeal at the court of appeals (although, one case was not taken there for review by the Department of Justice) in the health benefits conflict, and OPM also did extremely well in other policy areas at the higher court level.

The basic question here regarding the courts is, What are they doing second-guessing administrative decisions in personnel management? If the executive cannot manage itself on administrative matters, then government can never make sense. I have not done a systematic study, but it appears to me that the courts have begun to retreat from

micromanaging administrative decisions. The most important reason was the successful Reagan administration policy of choosing reasonable judges; but another may be that
the executive branch aggressively sought the right to manage itself, in the courts and before the public. Perhaps
OPM's victory before the Supreme Court, over whether the
government could run its charitable drive the way it thought
best, began to turn the tide. In any event, a government
administrator is not helpless even in the face of an activist
court if he aggressively presses the issue with higher-level
courts and is not reluctant to take his case to the public.

The Policymaking Process in the Bureaucracy

Perhaps the most mysterious aspect of government
administration is how the bureaucracy itself works. In theory, going back to Max Weber, the bureaucracy's job was to
provide the expertise. Expertise, of course, rests upon
doing sound analysis. Coming from an academic background, I was astonished at the poor quality of analytic
studies in government. Most did not even deserve the name.
One of the real accomplishments of the OPM political managers was to upgrade the quality of such studies by the
career staff. But much still needed to be done to make
them really useful. The basic problem is that the incentives are wrong.

Let me relate a true story to illustrate the problem. (As
Dave Barry would say, I'm not making this up!) The Merit
System Protection Board (MSPB)—the successor appeals
body to the Civil Service Commission—has a statutory
responsibility to study the operations of OPM. Each year it
released a "significant actions" report on OPM activities.
One year I was concerned about the quality of research in
these studies and referred them to MSPB's top political
leadership. In a sincere effort to improve the quality, they
called in an outside management consultant to teach
employees how to do better research and to communicate
it more effectively. Good start.

The consultant asked the staffers why they were doing such poor analysis, which they must have known was faulty. Right up until the end, they played dumb. But one of the more outstanding career employees—who told me this story—felt sorry for the consultant and finally told him the truth. The staff really did not want to produce sound analysis. Rather, the employees knew they had to produce reports that would satisfy OPM's critics in Congress. Otherwise, the critics would focus their fire on MSPB rather than OPM!

It was the consultant who learned the real lesson, that government expertise serves the interests of the bureaucracy, not objective policy analysis. But, as our dealings with MSPB—as with Congress, the courts, and the media— showed, creative confrontational political leadership can overcome the obstacles.

5

Reagan's Leadership

If the success of the Reagan administration came not from the smart guys in the White House or from the neutral experts in the "presidency," and success elsewhere depended upon whether or not there were committed people in the agencies, how did any coherence emerge? The answer is, through presidential leadership.

The American founders created a theory of government whereby political leadership could replace force. They reposed most of that leadership authority in a single person, the president, who was not to have the luxury of tyrannical power in exercising that leadership. Indeed, in *The Federalist Papers*, the authors set the very "objective of government" as protecting liberty's diversity, and they show how the Constitution provides the two other branches of government with powerful tools to check the president's power. The founders divided power so that it would not be abused, even though they knew leadership would be made more difficult.

Certainly, the president had his powers too. But to lead successfully, and at the same time not be tyrannical, he primarily had to rely upon, as Richard Neustadt called it, his "power to persuade." And that would depend upon his ability to exercise rather the skill of moral leadership than the tactics of force.

Political leadership is today complicated even further by the size and diversity of modern government. Not only is power shared by the legislative, executive, and judicial branches, but the executive branch itself is divided into countless agencies with different interests. There are four million military and civilian employees distributed into interest-protected enclaves, united only by their stake in a career system with relatively uniform benefits. To manage the four million, the president is given less than three thousand political appointees (and an additional thirteen hundred members of commissions with very limited power). Somehow he must rally the relative few to lead the four million, while Congress, the courts, the states, foreign affairs, organized interests, and media all pull in different directions.

What are the elements of successful presidential political leadership? Hedley Donovan, in his book *Roosevelt to Reagan* summarizes them by quoting long-time presidential adviser Bryce Harlow as saying, "Integrity is numbers one through ten." Donovan, elaborating, said that "today's president should look fair and be fair, be magnanimous, willing to give trust, and compassionate." He needs presence, dignity, a certain sense of distance, even mystery, and he must not be totally driven. He needs courage, both physical and moral. He needs to be self-confident, steady, and stable, with a sense of place.

Donovan then added "the ability to reduce complex issues to the essentials," and a sense of history. He said a president must offer vision and be able to communicate it. He needs a sense of humor and optimism, and a political philosophy hammered out in detail and tested intellectually and in experience. He needs to be curious and able to envision contingencies. It may be paradoxical, but the president must be flexible, pragmatic, and capable of compromise— as well as firm, decisive, and principled.

Moreover, said Donovan, a leader must be perceptive about people. "He must be shrewd enough to see when in-fighting is unavoidable, even useful, and when it is destruc-tive"; he must be willing to fire people. Finally, Donovan emphasized the need to keep track of what is delegated to subordinates and to have "a sense of priorities, for the country and in the use of his own time." He argued that a presidency, in this way, resembles a naval "watch."

How did Ronald Reagan fit Donovan's picture of a suc-cessful president? On character, Donovan mentioned him several times to illustrate this quality. Reagan's strength of moral character was manifest. But what about beliefs; was Reagan an ideologue? He did have strong beliefs, but he also could be pragmatic—indeed, many conservatives thought he was often too pragmatic. He seemed able to keep in balance a strong set of beliefs and an ability to compromise in the manner Donovan admired.

In 1980, Reagan defined his principles clearly and placed them before the public for acceptance or rejection in the election. When he won, Reagan took this public endorse-ment to Congress and was effective in getting his program approved. As economic difficulties deepened in 1982, the president shifted and made compromises. He rarely used his veto powers to confront Congress on basic principles.

In the 1984 election, Reagan did not campaign on a clear set of principles and as a result provided less successful leadership. At the insistence of White House aides Deaver, Darman, and Baker, he hoisted instead a standard of pastels. Consequently, when he tried to go before Congress to reduce spending, he could not persuade those tough legislators that he had a mandate. But he was resilient enough once again to rally Congress to pass the historic tax reform he had long desired. Overall, Reagan was rigid on some occa-sions, and flexible on others. He clearly had a philosophy, but he was flexible enough to modify it when necessary.

Some would argue that Ronald Reagan's weak point was people. He certainly did not keep track of everything assigned to people, nor did he fire anyone (except in the extreme case of my very disloyal deputy). Yet, he could be tough in turning from loyal subordinates when they were in trouble. Throughout his first term Ronald Reagan was criticized, especially by conservatives, for the top people he had appointed in the White House and the agencies. Clearly, he made mistakes. Gergen and Stockman have written that they neither respected the president's ideas nor felt bound to carry out his wishes. On the other hand, Reagan did appoint Watt, Donovan, Miller, Carmen, Pauken, and many others who did carry out his program. Most important, one of his most profound and enduring legacies—appointing a whole new judiciary with conservative members—was a personnel accomplishment. Without a large number of good people, he could not have been as successful as he was.

Ronald Reagan's strongest point was his ability to concentrate on essentials, to set priorities. He left most of the day-to-day administration of government to subordinates, while he kept his eye on a few key policies. On these, he certainly did follow up. Occasionally, as with the Iran-Contra policy, this method failed him. Yet his general approach, versus that of Jimmy Carter—who would even arrange the schedule for the White House tennis courts—allowed him to push a concentrated agenda.

This distinction between leadership and day-to-day management was forcefully brought home to me at a panel composed of Reagan administration management experts. We were celebrating the facts that we had introduced the first real cash-management system, had created effective collection techniques for bills past due, and had made the government's health insurance and retirement systems more rational. The total saved from these reforms was a reasonably impressive $40 billion or so over the five-year budget cycle; but it soon became clear that these mere dollar savings over a rather short period paled compared to those given priority by the president which transformed Washington's governmental landscape.

Five Reagan policies altered the New Deal welfare state system, pushing it toward his vision of freedom and federalism. They are the measure of his leadership. Three of these initiatives emanated directly from the president, and were constantly pushed by him, and two were seized upon as convenient means to achieve other long-held goals. The first was the 1981 budget. Before the institutional bureaucracy and the permanent government in OMB and Congress knew what had hit them, the Reagan budget was adopted, thereby cutting unnecessary projects and slashing fat from almost every existing program.

Virtually every domestic agency cut its staff by 5 percent or more, and a dozen cut by 10 percent or more. Five cut by 15 percent or more. Total controllable nondefense expenses were cut by 10 percent. Even the growth rate of entitlements was cut in half. By fiscal year 1986, entitlements had stabilized at 10.8 percent of GNP, and controllable domestic spending had declined from 4.8 to 3.8 percent of GNP. That first budget turned the tide against ever-growing government programs.

The second presidential initiative was an income tax rate cut of 23 percent to initiate Reagan's "supply-side" economic program to stimulate growth. As Professor Aaron Wildavsky of the University of California at Berkeley noted, before Reagan the tax take was about 19.6 percent of gross national product, compared with 19.3 percent four years afterward. How so little, with the 20 percent cut in tax rates? What happened was that Reagan cut what *would have been* tax increases caused by the "bracket creep" of inflation driving taxpayers into ever higher rate categories. Without Reagan, he shows, taxes would have been 23.8 percent of GNP. The bottom line of the Reagan tax reforms in the first term was that a monumental federal tax cut of 4.5 percent of GNP took place against that which otherwise would have been levied. In a five-trillion-dollar economy this is an *enormous* amount of money left in the hands of the people.

The Reagan initiatives would have dissipated had it not been for two other reforms, both originally opposed by Reagan's aides. The first was tax indexing—which finally took effect in 1986—proposed by Senator Bob Dole (R-Kans.), and ironically opposed by Don Regan's Treasury Department. This radical reform ended automatic tax increases caused by bracket creep. If Congress wanted more taxes, it would have to *vote* for them, instead of hiding behind automatic increases caused by inflation. This reform consolidated the earlier Reagan reforms and translated the original tax reductions into a *permanent* restraint on automatic increases in tax rates.

The next straw in breaking the New Deal's "tax and spend, spend and elect" policy was the spending limit proposed by Republican Senators Phil Gramm of Texas and Warren Rudman of New Hampshire, and Democratic Senator Fritz Hollings of South Carolina. This blunt instrument attacked the other half of runaway government—spending. In its first year it caused the first real across-the-board spending cut since 1981, and it additionally served as a real restriction on following budgets. By 1990 federal spending was lower by $470 billion (including the savings and loan bailout) than Congressional Budget Office 1985 projections for spending without GRH.

Finally, President Reagan forced a radically new tax program on the government. Rather than an income tax system with progressively higher taxing levels, a new system was created with basically four levels, set at moderate rates, the lower at 15 percent and the top level at 28 percent. The top marginal rate dropped from 70 to 33 percent. This represented the first time in history the progressive element in income tax rates had been flattened so dramatically by a democratic government. The corporate rate was also reduced (while also requiring a minimum tax from all).

This five-part revolutionary program shifted the political axis in Washington. President Reagan had not only the leadership vision to set the original course, but also the moral courage to accede to Dole and Gramm-Rudman-Hollings, which delivered the *coup de grace*. By assaulting the status quo with only five well-timed hammer blows, Ronald Reagan simply took the money away from the politicians and began to redirect it back to the people. As a result, he fundamentally changed the American government.

Like the bracket-creep tax increases that did not occur, the full impact of Ronald Reagan's leadership cannot be appreciated by looking just at the obvious government programs. In 1980 Ronald Reagan saw a problem that went beyond mere government. Both government and business had grown fat, lazy, and inefficient. America had entered a worldwide economy with American business resting on its 1950s lead over the rest of the world. By the 1970s, the world had caught up and America had not adjusted. Secure in the illusion that we did not have to compete, Americans were told they could spend their inheritance on more and more government programs.

The president's first act sent a signal to both government and the private sector—it froze government employment as a means to trim costs. Not only did this tell the federal establishment that he meant business, but it also was a signal to private sector leaders that they too could take radical steps to reinvigorate their companies. As government work reforms were instituted, especially making performance more important in pay and retention policy, these too sent a message.

One more bit of Irish luck prevailed. For decades, American unions had successfully fought measures to end inefficient work practices that protected unnecessary jobs. It was no different in government. So it was not surprising that the federal sector labor unions reacted to the Reagan hiring freeze and work practices reforms with threats of strikes, "job actions," and other harassment techniques. Several of these actions took place.

Then the unions went too far, and labor-management relations in the United States changed forever. On August 3,

1981, the union representing air-traffic controllers, PATCO, after extraordinary contract concessions by the government, violated the law and told its members to walk off their jobs and strike. But PATCO seriously misjudged Ronald Reagan. He fired every striker who left his station.

The decision to dismiss the striking controllers was a personal decision of the president. Most of his major advisers on the matter opposed his decision to issue an ultimatum to dismiss anyone who did not report for work that day. Even those of us who agreed with him favored reopening negotiations later. But the president said no. And American business leaders were given a lesson in managerial leadership they could not and did not ignore.

Many private sector executives have told me that they were able to cut the fat from their organizations and adopt more competitive work practices because of what the government did in those days. I would not be surprised if these "unseen" effects of this private sector shakeout under the inspiration of the president were as profound in influencing the recovery that occurred as the formal economic and fiscal programs. Perhaps they were more influential.

But the greatest indirect effect of Reagan's leadership was the dramatic change in the thinking of people around the world. For, fundamental changes in society arise from the way leaders change peoples' perceptions. By rejecting the message that the world economy and American society were stuck in what Jimmy Carter and most opinionmakers styled an "era of limits," and by adopting a relatively few major reforms in a blunt-instrument attack upon the status quo, Ronald Reagan led a reform of the economy, the government bureaucracy, and even foreign policy of historic dimensions. The result domestically was eighteen million net new jobs in the U.S. during the eight Reagan years, while Europe created no net new jobs at all. Worldwide, the Reagan example encouraged fifty-five nations to reduce their tax rates (compared with twenty-nine keeping them the same and only two increasing them, according to the *Wall Street Journal*). And to this must be added some role in promoting the worldwide rejection of the "evil empire" and communist rule.

Losing a few battles, like those David Stockman lamented on the budget, or Iran-Contra, pales next to the Reagan revolution in changing the world's way of seeing and governing itself. Against the odds, within his administration and without, Ronald Reagan made America and much of the world see his vision of freedom, federalism, and enterprise, and showed them how to follow in the path he blazed. That is leadership.

II

The Nature of the Bureaucracy

6

Changing Government Priorities

Getting Back to First Principles

Why had reform of the national government become such an issue for America by 1980? To Ronald Reagan, the answer was obvious: American government had strayed dangerously far from its constitutional roots. In the view of then-Governor Reagan, a large number of America's policy problems originated from a radical misunderstanding of the limited role of government in the context of American culture.

American politics once made a fundamental distinction between governmental decisions that are inherently coercive, and therefore to be limited, and the decisions of individuals—either freely through the exchange of goods in the economic market or through free commitments made in voluntary social arrangements—which should be maximized. The model of *The Federalist Papers* was that of a *federation* of the national government, state and local governments, voluntary associations, churches and businesses, which federation would provide self-reinforcing liberty and diversity for the whole society.

It was not until the twentieth century that we strayed from this view. Up to about 1900, government still spent only a small fraction of total wealth and less than 10 percent of public sector expenditures were made by the national and state governments combined.

However, a theory of government developed in Germany and Britain in the late nineteenth century was introduced to the United States by a group of Americans pursuing advanced studies in those countries. The essence of this imported theory, called "positive liberalism" or "welfare-state liberalism," held that reliance upon markets, free associations, and a preference for local versus national governments were useful, but not sufficient. Rather, the national government had to use its centralized powers positively to prioritize and reorder the general welfare. Positive liberalism argued that diversity and freedom created disorder, whereas central state direction could rationalize this disorder and more efficiently promote the welfare of all. For public administration, this welfare state meant the creation of a massive administrative apparatus at the national level.

Woodrow Wilson's critical contribution to this historic change was his argument that the political and administrative dimensions of government should be considered separately. Wilson argued that the great task of producing social justice through national governmental programs could be achieved by the use of neutral, "scientific" administrative methods. Values need not intrude into the debate at all because there was a neutral, scientific answer to most policy problems. America need not worry about a potentially tyrannical national government created by the welfare state because government would do only what the "science" of public administration deduced was proper.

To Woodrow Wilson, truly the American father of the modern liberal welfare state, it was "manifestly a radical defect in our federal system that it parcels out power and confuses responsibility." Wilson believed that all governments must have a single center of power to order what the nation should do. He believed the U.S. Constitution made a fundamental mistake by dividing power. The more power was divided, Wilson argued, the more it was prey to irresponsibility. Abuses of power could be controlled through the people—exercised in particular through their agent the president.

Wilson argued that *The Federalist Papers* had simply misapplied the British "model," which was supposed to be America's heritage, and that our Constitution should have been more sensitive to its history. What Wilson taught took hold during the creation of the twentieth-century American presidency.

To Reagan conservatives—inspired by professor Vincent Ostrom's critique of the British model—the 1980s crisis in politics and economics was largely the end result of the Wilsonian refusal to face the inevitable presence of political values in public policy and administration. To them, there could be no value-free public policy or administration. So they created a new—or rather went back to an old—theory of government administration based upon the federalist consensus of the founders. The president specifically stated that he intended to reestablish the debate over government "on the terms originally intended by the founders."

Ronald Reagan's interest in federalism as the first part of a theory of government reform was especially evident in his deregulation efforts and his successful block grant transfers of functions to state and local governments in 1981-82; and in continuing initiatives throughout his administration—some successful and some not—to transfer power back from the national to state and local governments.

Reestablishing the Federalist Principle in Personnel Administration

The Intergovernmental Personnel Act grant program was established a decade ago so the national government could "teach" states and localities how to manage people. The funding for IPA projects was to serve as seed money to encourage state and local governments to build systems of personnel administration and train staff in a wide range of bureaucratic tasks so they could become more like the federal government in Washington. To do this, OPM financed, on a joint basis with state and local governments, over five thousand personnel management grant and training projects at a cost to the federal government of over $160 million. Although it was never intended to be permanent, it seemed to have no end. I thought that it was exactly the type of program the Reagan administration was elected to eliminate.

I resolved to kill IPA quickly, before anyone could notice. Obviously, this could not be done through legislation since we would need action by both houses of Congress. The solution had to be to starve it. Therefore, during the transition, I resolved to defund the program in the first Reagan budget, with the hope it could not be revived thereafter. After a struggle with OMB, which wanted to keep a low level of funding, OPM was successful in zero-funding the grant program in the budget. Congress could not easily oppose this because it was such a small part of an overall total that overwhelmed them.

The repeal of the IPA grant program was a minor but significant step in carrying out the administration's policy of reducing the number of categorical grant programs and returning to state and local governments responsibilities that are properly theirs. In the context of the overall federal budget, the program was small, but this same argument is made for thousands of federal programs.

The revolutionary nature of the first two Reagan budgets, along with their related deregulation efforts, was that they sought out hundreds of small programs like IPA, which added up to billions of dollars, and eliminated or modified them. Moreover, for OPM, the elimination of the IPA grant program was a not insignificant saving of $20 million, representing 15 percent of our non-trust-fund budget.

The act also had set standards requiring states and localities to ensure the impartial and efficient administration of state and local government grant programs, which had much greater impact than the amount of money involved. Now I believed that the federal government was not run as well as most state and local governments. Who were we to tell them how to do things properly? State and local government misdeeds and inefficiencies are controlled better by their own citizens than by personnel standards promulgated in Washington. The states had already improved and modernized their personnel systems without much help from federal rules.

Yet, in 1981 fourteen states were forced by federal rules to run expensive dual personnel systems—one system to meet federal personnel requirements for grant-aided programs and another system for the rest of state government. In those states where there was a single system, there were frequently irrational restrictions as the result of federal standards, some of which—such as restricting the number of political positions—the bureaucracy could not impose upon the national government itself.

Congress, however, would not support our legislation to abolish the standards, so we liberalized the regulations—despite carping from members of Congress who were beholden to state and local government employee unions who used the federal standards to muscle state and local officials to gain benefits. In June 1982 OPM published new regulations, which simplified the standards from forty-three detailed pages of rules in the *Code of Federal Regulations*, to fewer than four pages.

In place of a cumbersome array of detailed merit-system requirements, the regulations consisted of only a list of principles which were merely recommended to be adopted by the state and local governments. Certification of compliance was to be made by the state governors and local chief executives themselves. No longer would OPM send its agents into the field in order to coerce state and local officials to comply with federal merit-system edicts. In the future, OPM would respond only to complaints. So by eliminating the grants and by transferring most of the administration to state and local governments, we had advanced the president's federalism and deregulation programs.

Even these modified rules proved troublesome. I had been warned by then-Congresswoman Geraldine Ferraro—head of one of OPM's oversight subcommittees—that I must implement her stricter view of the law. When I received a complaint about possible abuses of the standards in the 1984 election (when Ferraro was then a vice presidential candidate), I was attacked by three Democratic governors for even asking them for data to evaluate whether their programs met the remaining requirements. I took the opportunity to challenge these Democrats to join with me in eliminating the Intergovernmental Personnel Act completely. But they were too wedded to the Wilsonian idea of the centralized welfare state overseeing the states to help, even when they themselves were the objects of federal harassment.

Taking Charge of the Bureaucracy

The IPA program was by no means our only change in priorities. On April 12, 1981, the Democratic Speaker of the House, Tip O'Neill, was reported in the *Washington Star* as having said:

> Over the years I sneaked into the budget $45 million for a group of doctors who said they had a method to increase the height of dwarves from 26 to 48 inches. Another time I put in $18 million for experiments for treating knock-knees, another $12 million for turned-in ankles.
>
> But my philosophy of government belongs to bygone days. This cannot happen anymore. People now believe that gov-

ernment is bad and that's one of the troubles we Democrats are facing.

We must, therefore, admit to the mistakes we made and try to correct them. We over-regulated, we overspent, we overprogrammed, we were overfull of idealism. We brought into government too many from the world of universities and not enough people from business. We went too far with our emphasis on clean air and clean water and all that. It was too late when we began to realize that we were living in a world in which we had to tighten our belt. It is a very different world from the one I was brought up in.

Perceptions about policy were changing, and so were those about administration. In an early speech before the American Society of Public Administration, I described the second element of the Reagan theory of political administration. I challenged the intellectual foundations of Wilsonian administration and said we had to review our assumptions about government management. Whereas Wilson had blurred the distinction between policy and administration, Max Weber, the father of modern public administration, always made this a critical distinction. As Weber put it in his seminal *Politics as a Vocation*, the politician's calling is "to take a stand" on an issue, the civil servant's is "exactly the opposite principle, (that) of responsibility." He wrote:

> The honor of the civil servant is vested in his ability to execute conscientiously the order of superior authorities. Without this moral discipline and self denial, in the highest sense, the whole apparatus would fall to pieces.

In my speech, I said that we political executives in the new administration had a mandate from the electorate to reorient domestic programs to the private sector and local governments and that we intended to use the legitimate democratic power given to us to achieve that result. No longer would we follow the old approach summarized so well by Tip O'Neill. We knew from polls that most federal career officials disagreed with the direction we proposed to pursue, but we expected their support because we had the right to expect it.

I told these top career officials that they, more than most, knew the problems. I repeated the story of Mayor Ed Koch of New York complaining one time about overbearing federal government regulations. An aide responded, "But, Ed, you were a congressman for twelve years down in Washington, and a pretty liberal one. You voted for all the stuff you're complaining about now." Koch retorted, "Sure, who knew? We were crazy. We voted for a lot of junk. A lot of political and social theorists came in and told us what to vote for and we did." I promised those in the audience less "junk" to administer. Less government could be better and more efficient government, and more rewarding to those who managed it.

In attempting to win support and to set our claim to that support, I mentioned the havoc across the sea in our sister democracy Great Britain. British public sector unions were outraged by the policies of the new conservative government of Prime Minister Margaret Thatcher. William Kendall, the general secretary of the Council of Civil Service Unions, had moved into the administrative apparatus of the government. He called a strike that, he said, would "blow the government's economic strategy right off course." I noted that a similar call to action by a prominent American union leader was made to my audience earlier in the conference, but that this represented a shortcut to the end of a democratic society. I was confident the audience and federal employees generally would reject it and would support our right to lead in a new policy direction.

I pledged we would respect the rights of career civil servants by fairly enforcing the rules. We would take control and manage the government better, neither unnecessarily centralizing power in OPM, nor ignoring our responsibilities to correct merit-system abuses in the name of flexibility. We would stress bedrock public administration principles such as performance appraisal, performance pay, and merit systems. We would lead openly and systematically to show workers what was expected, and reward those who carried out their responsibilities efficiently. Moreover, we would take our fiduciary responsibilities seriously, such as the unfunded liabilities in the retirement system and a 75,000-case backlog in retirement claims for employees who had served faithfully but who were not receiving benefits because of bureaucratic delays at OPM.

I said we wanted career civil servants involved in policymaking, in spite of Weber's distinction. It was foolish to try to separate the responsibilities of political and career civil servants into airtight compartments. While columnist David Broder was correct in saying the Reagan administration did come to office with a more complete set of policy initiatives than any other he had seen in forty years or so of reporting on the scene, we needed very much the advice of the career civil servant who knew how the system really worked.

As a matter of policy, we did involve career officials. The professional associations in the public administrative area often characterized my leadership as excluding the views of career appointees. The truth was that those career employees who actually worked for me and with me probably thought my political appointees involved them too much. At OPM, we were constantly challenging the career staff to come up with more facts and new ideas. The political appointee simply cannot survive if he does not know the facts and have alternative ideas on how to solve policy problems, and the only repository of that institutional memory is the career service. As Weber said, that is its very soul.

I hired one political appointee from Capitol Hill who said, after his first exposure to OPM's policy-debate meetings, it was like going from Sparta to Athens—the difference between a congressman's dictatorial "This is what we are going to do; you guys get out of here and do it" and four and a half hours of vigorous debate, involving an agency head, over which policy direction OPM should follow.

Yet, at the end of the debate, someone had to make a decision, and that had to be the political appointee, especially if policy was to change. For the career staff necessarily represents the status quo. Both democratic theory and American law give the authority for change to the political appointee. Ultimately, he makes the decision, not the "neutral" career staff. Even our severest critics, like Professor Murray Camerow, were forced to concede that the political appointee must have the final word, even if these critics were unwilling to arrive at the logical conclusion that our new theory of political administration was sound.

Learning Management from the Private Sector

With its emphasis upon the importance of the private sector, it was natural for the Reagan administration to add business management theory as its third principle of administration. One book popular at the time symbolized to us what government needed to do to become more efficient. *In Search of Excellence*, by Thomas J. Peters and Robert H. Waterman, Jr., noted these major characteristics of well-managed organizations:

1. First and foremost, there is a bias for action. There is a do-it, try-it, fix-it mentality that solves problems quickly with a minimum of yack and number-crunching. These organizations do not wait, e.g., they create their own marketplace. They encourage experimentation and tolerate failure.

2. They are learning organizations: they listen, emphasize satisfying needs of their audience, are receptive to new ideas.

3. They are organized for entrepreneurship. These organizations encourage employees at all levels to be creative, and take practical risks. They treat employees as adults, giving responsibility, praise, and respect. They try to make the average person a hero: they reward him for his performance.

4. These organizations have simple structures and lean staffs. Top level staffs are small, and the concentration is on line operating units which fulfill the essential goal of the organization.

5. They concentrate their goals. They stick to their knitting, e.g., "never acquire a business you don't know how to run." They have a purpose and follow it.

6. These organizations balanced centralization and decentralization. They create an almost radical decentralization and autonomy, messiness around the edges. This lack of tight coordination breeds the entrepreneurial spirit. But this must be balanced with firm controls on budget, personnel, and the other quality things that count in the goal of that organization.

The most essential management activity found in this study of American business was the ability to create an environment in which leaders could make decisions and act. With government's bias in favor of inaction, we thought this insight applied especially to us. McKinsey and Company's British managing director, J. Roger Morrison, found this ability to make changes the reason for management success in Great Britain: "They either had to fight to survive or go bust." Our general feeling was that an emphasis upon action and a need to respond to change were healthy correctives for a timid government administration.

On the other hand, it was clear that productivity was related to a positive attitude toward employees, one of the Peters and Waterman measures of success. Such techniques as careful attention to employee concerns can help in good management. Human resource development through training and positive employee relations was considered a critical aspect of good management. But the feeling was strong among the early Reagan management team that Peters and Waterman had defined the primary factor: action.

Ralph Z. Sorenson, former professor at the Harvard Business School, college president, and president of Barry Wright Corporation, influenced us too with his definition of what kind of leadership we needed.

> What matters most is to have reasonably intelligent, hardworking managers who have a sense of pride and loyalty toward their organization; who can get to the root of a problem and who are inclined toward action; who are decent human beings with a natural empathy and concern for people; who possess humor, humility, and common sense; and

who are able to couple drive with stick-to-it-iveness and patience in the accomplishment of a goal. One must have an ability to express oneself, possess leadership skills, have courage and a strong sense of identity, and have the ability to make positive things happen.

Mortimer Finberg and Aaron Levenstein's advice to go beyond simple data or analytical reasoning and rely on experience-based, good commonsense intuition influenced us too.

We believed that the compensation system, as the principal incentive system, should be generous enough to get the job done, including making certain the employee thinks he is fairly compensated. But we also believed that an employer wastes corporate resources if he overcompensates employees (a point made in Bruce R. Ellig's *Executive Compensation*). Overcompensation leads to a slack rather than a taut work force. Staying competitive with those in the market for the same employees made sense to us. We even paid somewhat more to obtain a competitive edge for critical skills. But unnecessarily attractive salaries and benefits simply were deemed irrational.

We believed that the government channeled too much of its compensation into retirement rather than current salary, relative to the private sector. It was biased against younger employees, and also focused too much psychic energy toward the future, leading to retirement at first eligibility for valued senior employees. My personal observation was that an obsessive focus upon retirement in the federal government blunted our employees' drive to face and enjoy the many challenges which make work rewarding. We believed in a balance between short- and long-term compensation policies.

Most private sector management gave salary increases to employees based upon performance and not seniority. Where seniority use was widespread there usually was a history of labor unrest and later unionization. More progressive firms like IBM and Pfizer gave raises on the basis of performance only. We accepted as axiomatic that any pay-for-performance system must be based upon a solid performance appraisal system. We recognized from private sector performance, however, that a performance appraisal system is always evolving and is never perfect. It is necessary to achieve a reasonable level of reliability, then to implement and upgrade the system, and finally to provide consequences for the system. Without consequences, the system would degenerate into a paper exercise and become useless.

The Reagan management team was also concerned with the growth of supervisory staff, especially in the areas of finance, personnel, and materials acquisition. These areas must be covered by staff organizations, and efficient staff-control mechanisms can make the difference between the survival and the failure of an organization. But this evident need for staff often leads to an overreliance upon it relative to line functions.

Peter F. Drucker estimated that at many large private sector manufacturing companies, staff had grown five to ten times as fast as the number of operating people in production, engineering, research, sales, and customer service. In addition, he found that in many companies, the middle— between the first line supervisor and the corporate top— had been growing three or four times faster than sales, even before adjustment for inflation. He believed that in small and medium-size companies, the growth may have been faster. Our evidence was that this growth in government was even higher. Charles Peters called this phenomenon "slot inflation." He recounted a story of Ellis O. Briggs, then the ambassador to Czechoslovakia. Briggs ordered two thirds of the embassy staff cut only to find that the embassy then became the most efficient one in the service. When Phil Keller and Ann Cooper compared the U.S. embassies in Morocco and Mali, they found that the latter had a staff less than half the size of the former and was the more efficient. When the District of Columbia reduced garbage crews from four men to three, the result was not less but greater productivity.

Drucker's solution was to consolidate jobs that had grown over time. These positions were created at first for good reasons. At some point they became overspecialized and the new positions simply took on a life of their own. One solution was to combine two jobs. Or, as jobs became vacant through retirement, death, and resignation, leave them open for six or eight months and see what happened. Unless there was an overwhelming clamor to fill the job, abolish it. Most important, he suggested using attrition to consolidate levels of management that had grown over time. Such multiple levels slowed the decision process and made the organization increasingly incapable of adapting to change.

Drucker suggested that each time staff demanded a new task, it should be forced to abandon an old one. Staff should be given specific goals and objectives and held responsible for them. Regular evaluation on a three-year cycle should be used to determine whether staff work is necessary. Finally, he suggested that staff work should be not a career but only a part of a career. True management should be rotated through different functions performed by the firm, always with an eye on the central goal of the organization.

A related phenomenon was the growth of subunits within organizations. Large organizations do have benefits, but they also have weaknesses. Of the publicly held American companies having a hundred thousand or more employees in 1970, twelve showed employee declines in the succeeding decade, and only five showed gains of 10 percent or more. Size is not necessarily more efficient. It is a commonplace that innovation comes primarily from small-sized firms. This creative spirit can be developed to some degree within large organizations, however, by decentralizing functions to smaller-size units with more clearly focused goals. This has the substantial side effect of cutting down on alienation. And if size was a problem for the private sector, we believed it was a greater one for the mammoth federal government.

The idea that drove us most was that performance was the essence of personnel management in the private sector. A survey of chief executive officers in the private sector asked them to order ten elements of good management practice. Overwhelmingly, the need for performance was ranked number one. If one idea was lacking in government, it was that performance should be first.

These management ideas dominated the thinking of the Reagan management team, especially at OPM, but also—through our coordinating councils—throughout the government. Most Reagan appointees had come from the private sector and many were successful there. It was natural that we would take these ideas into government with us. And they did help us manage better.

But it was not quite the same.

7

Government Is Different

Government Management and the American Culture

Roy Ash, when he was director of OMB, explained to private sector executives the difference between government and private management by using this illustration of the public sector administrative environment:

> Imagine that you were the chief executive officer of your company and that the board of directors was made up of your customers, your suppliers, your employees, and your competitors, and that you required a majority vote on everything. Wouldn't you conduct your business in a different way than you do now? Going from the private to the public sector is not going from the minor leagues to the major leagues in baseball; it is like going from softball to ice hockey.

Dean Sayre of Columbia University summarized it this way: "There are many similarities between public and private administration—all of them trivial." More seriously, Richard Cavanaugh of McKinsey and Company specified the major differences as follows:

First, *the staff is the line.* Over sixty line executives report to the president, many of whose agencies perform overlapping functions. The size of the staff, in turn, forces more reliance upon coordinating staffs.

Second, *the process is the substance.* Because of the massive complexity and interdependence of government—he points to two thousand product lines or programs—coordinating processes becomes the only hope for comprehensive and rational decisionmaking. But, at the same time, this straitjackets initiative. The line manager's "carefully reasoned memo to his boss is cleverly summarized in a cover note by staff, and is relegated to Tab 21 in the briefing book."

Third, *managers don't manage.* Government executives are first and foremost representers—salesmen of ideas and rhetoric, and defenders of programs and jurisdiction. They spend a hugh amount of their time testifying before Congress, giving speeches, representing the agency to the central staff organizations, and being briefed in a short period of time on very complex issues. "Strategic" tends to become this session of Congress, this budget cycle, this press conference, now. The incentives in this environment are rather for initiating new programs than for managing existing ones.

Finally, *there are no politically neutral decisions.* "Politics ain't beanbag," he concludes; but "it isn't business administration, either."

Frank Carlucci explained the essential management principles from the perspective of the quintessential career public servant. First, there must be a cooperative staff relationship, especially between the key political and career staff. Second, because of the political environment, organizational changes must be made quickly, or they will be frustrated. Third, the right people must be recruited or moved to the right job for each manager. Fourth, the successful public executive must create the impression of change or he will lose the initiative. Fifth, one must court Congress by being honest and doing his homework. Sixth, one must be decisive and gutsy.

These facts about the government management environment made it apparent to the Reagan management team that we could not simply copy private sector practices. Even the advice of competent public executives like former defense secretary Carlucci was not fully applicable to political executives. After all, career executives have the protection of the civil service rules and have an immunity from the media resulting from their presumed professionalism and lower visibility. So political executives need a fourth principle: that the fundamental difference in public administration is that it is public! It is scrutinized by Congress, the media, interest groups, and the public. It is life in a fishbowl full of sharks.

At one time government officials were admired and given deference but by the 1980s public administration was taking place in a sea of popular distrust. Public opinion polls clearly showed that large majorities did not like government: they believed that federal employees worked less, were better paid, and had better benefits than people in the private sector. To some extent this hostility represented the traditional healthy American distrust of government power. To some extent, the perceptions were true, and to some extent, the perceptions were very wrong. It was true, for example, that federal benefits tended to be substantially higher and that federal pay was somewhat more. It was also true that federal employees worked less effectively; but it was not true that it was the fault of the employees. We recognized that the bureaucratic system they worked under, plus the attitudes it generated, was the problem, not the people.

Even normally positive employer actions in the private sector become public relations problems for the government and demand tougher political attitudes. For example, each year at a ceremony I hosted we had the president bestow honorific and monetary recognition upon the government's top career executives. Our reward was a newspaper article on the awards ceremony headlined, "Some U.S. Executives Given $10,000 Each," with a story suggesting that these "bureaucrats" did not deserve that much. A television interviewer trapped me after the awards ceremony in 1982 and, with camera rolling and lights blazing, demanded to know how I could justify such bonuses "with so many poor Americans now out of jobs?" You can't win.

Likewise, when the Washington Redskins won the Super Bowl, I gave employees time off to watch the victory parade. Good employee relations? Yes. But we received harsh criticism from private sector employees who were not given the same break. In Washington, simple morale building can result in attacks on employee morale.

I knew we had a good work force but was convinced that its corporate structure and philosophy of doing business needed fundamental reform. Both structure and philosophy were biased against action, did not encourage listening, frustrated initiative, did not emphasize sticking to essential functions, were neither lean in staff nor simple in form, rewarded too little for performance, deferred compensation too long, and were too centralized on staff and too decentralized on line functions.

The American people were certainly ready for bureaucratic reform: in one poll, two thirds of Americans, in ranking twenty-six occupations in order of efficiency, put government dead last. Drucker concluded that "nobody believes any more that government delivers. Looking at modern states . . . I see government obese and muscle-bound and having lost its capacity to perform."

What had happened? Drucker said, "In the nineteenth century nobody worried much about government's capacity [to perform] because it did little and did it well." Prior to the 1930s in the United States, the federal government did not intrude greatly into people's lives. There were the post office, the military, and a federal bureaucracy whose work was confined to government activities that seldom brought it into contact with the average American citizen. And that was about it.

With the onset of the Great Depression and the New Deal the entire concept of what the federal government should do, could do, and how it would be done, changed. The New Deal set the national government's role as feeding, housing, clothing, educating, and otherwise caring for every aspect of people's lives. The government started to grow and never stopped. For each new problem there was a new agency. Soon, nearly every facet of American life could be touched by government bureaucracy.

With the power to act centered in Washington, with conflicts between programs and layers of red tape, centralized government did a great deal, but did it not very well. We believed the solution to better government was smaller government, particularly local and state government, better organized under dedicated political leaders, and privatizing what should not be done by government at all.

But my immediate responsibility was to make the national government work better. In fiscal year 1982 the federal government spent about $100 billion on administration, 78 percent of which went to its 2.1 million employees in 24,500 installations worldwide, working under 2,000 programs organized around 677 management systems. To coordinate this far-flung operation, 30 percent of the work force was strictly administrative or clerical. If its size and complexity were not enough to frustrate coordination and efficiency, civil service rules, devised to provide stability and protection, immunized the internal operations of agencies from initiative and created disincentives for good work practices.

By the 1980s poor management practices were rampant. Pay increases for over 90 percent of the federal work force were automatic and given to all based on length of service. Layoffs were based on seniority, not performance. Generous pensions created incentives to retire rather than work, with present pay discounted against long-awaited retirement. Pension payments were so attractive, especially for executives, that employees were almost *forced* to retire just when they reached their most productive ages. Other incentives led employees to perform too much overtime. Few were rewarded as they should be and few were disciplined. As a result, a survey of federal workers found that a majority did not feel they would be held responsible for unsatisfactory work.

Yet government career executives and their camp-followers in the schools of public administration vigorously supported this system, and even publicly argued that government employees should not be evaluated based upon how well they performed! About halfway through my term, at a meeting of government and academic management experts, I tried the shock treatment. I announced that the administration was giving up on trying to make government more efficient. Without cracking a smile, I said there had been too much opposition from the Congress, too much trouble from the unions, too much trouble from federal employees. "Let's take performance out of the government completely. It seems the only rational way to proceed after all of the complaints I have received."

I continued, "The first thing we should do is to get rid of the bonuses for the senior executive service. There have been complaints about bonuses already. Many career executives would be glad to get rid of them. Of course, many of our best executives—some sitting in this room—would have to leave government if that happened, but maybe that would not be the end of the world.

"Next we would get rid of merit pay. If you listen to my opponents, there should be a great cheer resounding from the hundred thousand managers covered by the merit pay system throughout the government. It might be a little hard on the thirty-five thousand better-performing managers, who were getting two pay-steps above what they would have gotten under the old, automatic, seniority system. But, perhaps we should say 'the heck with them,' too.

"And if we got rid of more performance-based actions, we could then get rid of promotions. Seem reasonable? Promotions are rewards for performance, right? We would have no reason to reward the two hundred fifty thousand employees who receive promotions for good performance each year right now.

"That's my new plan," I said. "No more merit, no more of that. We'll just let everybody do what he wants to do. We'll rotate management positions around or something. It will be a really wonderful system with automatic increases based upon seniority for everyone.

"And look at the great things this would do. Primarily, it would drive out the competitive, hard-charging people who now work for the government. I mean, what do we need them for anyway? Let us have a nice system of nice people who are just getting along, but not doing much work because they are not rewarded."

Even my audience recognized that performance needed some emphasis in the federal government. When we talk about rewarding risk and extra effort, we are talking about a way of viewing human behavior which is deeply rooted in our American culture, our institutions, and our traditions. It speaks to the entrepreneurial character of Americans, even those who work for the government, perhaps primarily them because they feel its lack the most. One of the true tragedies of federal government employment is that its slack system seems to crush the human spirit. I cannot tell how many people I know in the government who admit little purpose in work other than a retirement check, one perhaps twenty years away. They receive no challenge from their work. It is sad that the worst victims of the system are the ones the employee lobbies say they are protecting.

Peter Drucker's book, *Innovation and Entrepreneurship*, sums up the importance of changing this government thinking and the existing structure: "To build entrepreneurial management into the existing public-service institution may...be the foremost political task of this generation."

Good personnel management systems based upon entrepreneurial performance cannot replace market discipline, or decentralization to inherently more efficient local governments; but for the national government they're the next best tool. And, much as the federal government needs to be reduced, it will, reduced or not, be with us a long time. The alternatives of government management are simple—effective political direction of a smaller, performance-oriented government work force; a "nice system of nice people" not being challenged by much of anything and wasting resources; a return to a spoils or patronage system and no civil service at all. If the present system cannot be reformed along the lines of the first alternative, the political administration solution, Americans will have to endure a wasteful and unresponsive government.

8

Making Personnel
Management Work

Making Performance Central

An idealist coming from the private sector to run a government agency typically might turn to a public administration textbook to determine how to manage his new
organization. He would assume that experts would at least
provide some guidelines. He would be disappointed, for
this is not possible in Washington. There any attempt to
manage the bureaucracy runs into the very different
"laws" of political trench warfare. As one who tried to
follow the maxims of my favorite public administration
text, I know.

Public Personnel Administration, by O. Glenn Stahl, lists
the rules for sound public personnel management. On the
basic question of how to compensate employees, the text
says, "Certainly the widespread custom of automatic increases without relation to performance has little to commend

it from the standpoint of good administration...to recognize meritorious achievement with accelerated increases is the preferred approach."

In addition, Stahl states that salaries for government executives are lower than those in the private sector, but that they equaled or exceeded the "prevailing [market] pay at lower...more routine levels." Ultimately, says Stahl, pay must be set based upon the "needs of the private sector, especially short supply." When supply is short, he suggests "special pay based upon market conditions."

Of retirement systems, Stahl criticizes cost- rather than reserve-based retirement systems with large unfunded liabilities, and specifically notes that "the holding power of a retirement system can also be a major deterrent, especially in those instances where the individual has already built up considerable credit in one system that is neither transferable nor available to him as a deferred annuity...if he should leave."

Stahl also holds that temporary appointments are "essential to a flexible personnel system," and that "a task of government management is to avoid the Scylla of a stagnant service while steering clear of the Charybdis of inordinate instability."

Each of these textbook principles was translated into personnel reform proposals by the Reagan administration. We began efforts to make performance the central element in the personnel system—implementing a performance appraisal system for the entire work force, creating a pay-for-performance system for managers, making proposals to extend pay for performance to all— basing career selections upon merit, providing pay and benefits at market rates, having a retirement system that was better funded and more flexible, and generally providing a balanced personnel system. Was OPM praised by those who had been advocating these reforms? With a few notable exceptions, no. No good government act went unpunished. Even Stahl spoke out against our reforms!

For the reader uninterested in the details of personnel administration, that is all you need to know and you can safely skip both the rest of this chapter and the next.

Perhaps no other theme dominated our Reagan administration personnel management reforms more than the one to make performance the central element of the personnel system. Remember that the Reagan administration was simply following the trail blazed by its predecessor, the Carter administration. To a great degree, President Carter had been elected because of his promise to reform the bureaucracy. He delivered, with the Civil Service Reform Act of 1978, ushered through Congress by the first OPM director, Alan Campbell. As was true of many of the limited number of its successes, the Carter administration did not get credit for this real bureaucracy reform.

One central principle of CSRA was that pay and retention be based upon performance. As part of its implementation apparatus, the CSRA provided for a modern, sound performance appraisal system. This was to replace the one established under the Performance Rating Act of 1950, which had become an automatic-pay-increase system under which more than 98 percent of employees were ranked at the same "satisfactory" performance rating. This was not a serious system and was so treated by managers and employees alike. The new CSRA system was to have multiple levels of evaluation and to be based upon sound definitions of work and performance following the best private sector models. The Carter administration began preparing for implementation immediately after the passage of the act in October 1978.

The 1980 election intervened, so it was left to the Reagan administration to implement the proposals by the statutory implementation deadline of October 1, 1981. And we did it. The Reagan administration began implementation as soon as I was appointed as civil service transition team leader in early November 1980. We had planned for it as

early as 1979, when I began transition planning. By the
legal implementation date, almost 90 percent of federal
employees—1.7 million— had been delivered performance
elements and standards, a remarkable achievement by the
Reagan management team, political and career. In addition, we placed over a hundred thousand executives and
managers under a new, more scientific appraisal system
and began to pay bonuses to those career managers who
performed well.

Once the new system was in place, over the next four
years OPM emphasized upgrading performance elements
and standards and changing the attitudes of management
and supervisors. After so many years of perfunctory ratings, all had to be trained to rate employees in a serious
manner. Employee reaction to the new system was remarkably positive. The Federal Employee Attitude Survey found
in 1983 that a majority of federal employees believed the
performance elements of their new performance appraisal
system were fair. Moreover, management did learn to dis-
tribute performance rankings better, spreading ratings
among three rating positions, although ratings were skewed
to the upper end of the rating system with very few at the
two less satisfactory rating levels. After many years of abuse,
this was not surprising. Even among managers, 65 percent
of the ratings were at the two highest levels: "exceeds fully
successful" and "outstanding." Extremely few ratings were
at the "unsuccessful" or "minimally successful" level. Thus,
even after four years of effort, performance distributions,
while better spread, left much to be desired.

At OPM itself we made remarkable progress: the number
of outstanding ratings went down from 43 to 6 percent and
the "fully successful" standard for work became the average
rating. Other agencies, notably the Department of Commerce, made progress too. Yet, even in the best cases (OPM
included), there were few at the "unsuccessful" rating.
Going that far was more revolutionary than the bureaucracy could stand. It was possible to train supervisors to
distinguish between levels of satisfactory performance, but

the civil service culture was too strong to admit that some employees were unsuccessful, and thus very few were failed.

A major feature of the CSRA was the requirement to establish merit pay systems covering management officials in grades GS-13 through GS-15 of the general schedule, and the Senior Executive Service. This substantial change in pay policy marked the first time that federal pay increases would be directly related to performance rather than to longevity. This is just what the textbooks called for. But it was not to happen without bureaucratic shenanigans.

Without notice, the comptroller general (exercising his role as one of the power centers of the bureaucracy) ruled— a mere three weeks before the new pay system was due to be implemented—that there would be one-third fewer dollars in the merit pay pool than the Carter administration had calculated. I immediately received pressure from GAO, the unions, and executive and professional associations, saying that the new system would not work and should be abandoned. The rumor was that this, indeed, had been the purpose behind the GAO decision.

Even with this serious loss of money to fund the merit bonuses, I considered it essential to proceed with implementation, or else there never would be pay for performance in the federal government. Yet the GAO ruling reduced the merit pay fund so much that I was forced to grant full comparability increases to all covered employees, and was left with only a very small pool available for the merit awards. But we did establish this first large scale pay-for-performance program in the civil service, which allowed the idea to be extended later.

The pay-for-performance system for the Senior Executive Service (SES) also ran afoul of Washington's fishbowl management environment. Here, instead of a pool, a straight bonus-for-performance system was established. This made the scheme immune to GAO nitpicking. Yet there were other political roadblocks. The original CSRA allowed up to 50 percent of SES career executives to receive bonuses. When, under the Carter administration, the National Aeronautics and Space Administration paid out bonuses to almost half of its employees (46 percent), Congress became concerned that the bonus program would be abused by agencies giving bonuses to half of their executives in one year and to the other half the next. The Carter lobbyist told me the real reason for the protest was that congressional staffs were not eligible for bonuses and therefore tried to kill the program for the executive branch. In any event, Congress passed an amendment to a supplemental appropriation act to restrict the number of bonuses to 25 percent, which Carter's OPM later limited to 20 percent. Still, 20 percent was a reasonable figure, and, indeed, the agencies over the next four years paid out bonuses to even less than that maximum.

The Reagan administration encouraged the granting of bonuses, including the Presidential Rank Awards, which recognized a very small number of highly exceptional executives with bonuses of $10,000 and $20,000. The administration believed that if career executives performed well they should be rewarded for it. Approximately six thousand career executives were rewarded with bonuses over the four years of my term. Because of our responsible administration of the bonuses, Congress removed entirely the restriction on the percent eligible and OPM set a new limit at 30 percent. Somewhat later, the administration supported legislation that transformed the SES bonus into a pool concept, since that system had now become acceptable through successful OPM-supported modifications to the managerial pay pool plan. So pay for performance for executives was actually implemented successfully in the first Reagan term, a rare gain in an environment so comfortable with mediocrity.

The CSRA had created the Senior Executive Service to become a separate personnel system based upon the principle of performance. Not only would pay become based more on performance, but the CSRA allowed agencies to create executive positions on their own authority, without having to go through OPM to define the positions, as was required under the old, more rigid, pre-Carter system. The

CSRA also removed the need to prove in a hearing that transfers of SES executives to different positions were in the government's interest, a legal requirement which became so burdensome that few transfers were made before CSRA. The new procedures allowed managerial discretion and resulted in better use of personnel. In one case, I transferred an uncooperative executive—who had been in the same position so long he could not consider our new ideas—to a new position where he became one of my most valuable leaders. Over the four years, approximately one thousand reassignments were made at the executive level under the supervision of Executive Resource Boards, which consisted of the highest-level noncareer and career executive leadership of the agencies. Other organizational changes began to be made with management needs in mind, and made without being inhibited by fear of legalistic delays. These reforms must seem simple to private sector executives who take them for granted, but they represented significant gains for effective management in a government that actively encouraged legalistic form over the substantive task of getting the work performed efficiently.

In some agencies, resistance to the new system was of heroic dimensions. The least political of the good government reforms of the first Reagan administration was an evaluation system to see how well, or poorly, the different agencies of the government were performing. The president expected reliable performance data to aid him in managing his executive branch through the quality of performance evaluations, the spread of performance ratings, the distribution of merit-based bonuses, the number of work hours his employees performed, and many other indicators of good management performance. He found that the outdated management evaluation tools that existed in the government provided no real answers.

So we at OPM began asking the agencies to supply data, both to our central data system and to the agencies' own management systems. Incredibly, the agencies were not even collecting basic management data for their own internal use. The resistance from the bureaucracy to providing this simple data was intense. The agencies simply did not like the idea of *anyone* looking at how they were performing.

More incredibly, the agency responsible for evaluating OPM's actions, the Merit Systems Protection Board, actually objected to OPM's reform. MSPB said that by providing statistical data, detailed information on individual government bureaus would be lost. The problem with studying only individual government bureaus for OPM was that we had reviewed so few of them that we had no picture of how the whole government was performing. In any rational division of responsibility, each agency should evaluate its own performance for small units and MSPB would review those actions. But we felt a central management agency like OPM should have a governmentwide perspective, derived from broad statistical data from major subunits of the government.

MSPB, however, liked the single-installation studies because they helped MSPB do its job of overseeing the merit system. MSPB realized it was easier to pressure OPM to enforce standards than it was for MSPB to force the whole government to respond to them. Moreover, criticizing OPM was fair game, and to do so on a minor subject like evaluation did not draw any real blood. And so it did. The new evaluation system was still only partially in operation at the time I left government.

The foregoing was small-time stuff. In 1982 OPM proposed to extend the pay-for-performance concept to non-management employees and to give performance points for retention during layoffs. This created a firestorm. The OPM plan was to use regulatory authority to standardize performance appraisal systems throughout the white collar work force. It then would link the ratings more closely to so-called within-grade pay increases, now to be based directly upon performance, and to the existing awards system, which operated largely independently of performance ratings.

Likewise, the reduction-in-force (RIF) procedures were to be amended to rank performance above seniority, so the best performers would be saved during layoffs. The proposal would also limit "bump and retreat" procedures in RIFs, which allowed employees to move down to lower and lower levels in the bureaucracy so they could hold on to any job, no matter how low the job, no matter how overqualified they were. Not only did this displace other lower-level employees who might be performing better, but because of federal procedures that did not allow pay to be reduced this also resulted in high-ranking executives bumping down to perform routine clerical work while still receiving $50,000 annual salaries. OPM's proposal was also aimed at protecting well-performing women and minority employees, who suffered most from the "last hired, first fired" aspect of the previous RIF procedures because they had less seniority.

The response from the unions was especially forceful. They declared that seniority must be fully protected, whatever the cost. But OPM worked with members of Congress and representatives of employee associations to achieve an acceptable compromise. The final regulations moved the *Federal Times*, the publication for federal employees, to note that "weeks of negotiation" produced a proposal which was "by far the most acceptable to the many groups involved." It noted that "members of Congress are impressed with how far OPM seems to have compromised." The headline was that OPM was able to "satisfy its foes."

The liberal *Washington Monthly* commented:

> Indifference to performance is not an abstract problem of public administration. It is central to the declining efficiency of both American industry and government. . . . The Reagan administration, to its great credit, is trying to do something about this, trying in the words of one official, "To make job performance the center of the federal personnel system." Neo-liberals will support this effort.

Despite broad support for the proposal, the unions refused to budge and they and their OMB supporters were able to get their allies in Congress to pass an appropriation rider forbidding expenditures of funds to implement the OPM proposal.

The administration continued working with Congress, and it was not until after I left the office that a further modified pay-for-performance system for all employees was finally enacted.

What did the employees think of their union's efforts? An MSPB survey of federal employees found that 83 percent did not think the performance appraisals were manipulated to affect RIF results, the primary complaint of the unions. The data showed that 88 percent of federal employees believed in giving job performance great weight in a RIF, and a large majority believed that performance should be important in making pay decisions. Employees wondered whether such rules could be implemented fairly—employees were to be rated by career, not political supervisors, contrary to the union propaganda about "politicized" performance decisions—but they supported the basic idea.

A survey in *Working Woman* found that more than 60 percent of Americans generally, with a majority in all demographic groups, want a job where pay is tied to performance. This is an expectation so widespread in the United States that it was difficult to see what the unions' argument was about. Almost all American workers are evaluated based upon their performance. Why not government employees too?

Why were our reforms to make performance central so difficult to implement? Political scientists have long known that those most interested in an issue create the most pressure. The federal unions and employee associations were very interested, especially the malcontents that tend to dominate them at the shop level in the domestic agencies. They wrote often to newspapers and congressmen, and even contributed funds to congressmen. Indeed, the fastest growing political action committees are federal employee PACs. But the basic fact of life in Washington is that there is no equivalent force for good government per se. Once while I was arguing for my pay-for-performance regulations with a senator with hundreds of thousands of federal employee constituents, he replied, "This is a great idea. My experience in the executive branch says this is exactly what is needed. Of course, I have to oppose you." He was up for reelection.

Even the simplest and most necessary reforms—which would never be issues in the private sector—became politicized. Employee groups easily created roadblocks to good government reforms by pressuring Congress. No one else knew or cared enough to play a countervailing role in Congress. The Grace commission and the Public Service Research Council tried, but they were no match for the intense activities of our employee associations which thought performance standards would ruin government.

Restoring Merit to the Buddy System

Over 90 percent of the mid- and upper-level positions in the federal government are filled by one employee requesting another by name. How can this take place under the civil service's merit system? Unfortunately, the old merit examination for government employment is dead.

During the Reagan administration, there was not even an entrance exam for college graduates who desired to enter the civil service. There used to be one, but Jimmy Carter's people (at the Department of Justice, not OPM) made a sweetheart court settlement with minority interest-group representatives to end the Professional and Administrative Career Examination (PACE). PACE did not discriminate against anyone, except in skills and ability, but more whites passed the exam than blacks or Hispanics. And that, during the Carter era, was called discrimination. Tough luck if in the process the government could not test for merit. But merit was damaged long before PACE.

What replaced the merit system? The buddy system. With no examinations—or what amounted to the same thing, the widely used "credentials exams," which do not differentiate very well—why not pick friends or relatives? The law forbids nepotism, but it does not forbid referring your child or spouse to another buddy, who will hire the relative through using an exam that scores almost everyone the same, and then request the relative by name from the "examination" score list.

Statistical probability theory posits odds of about fifty to one against an individual being picked for government work. The odds against two individuals being chosen in the same nuclear family are about five hundred to one. The odds against three are vast. How many two- or three- or even four-member families do you know that are working for the government? The odds against that are millions to one. Of course, the odds are much lower in Washington since it is the seat of the government. Yet the number of members of the same family employed here is far beyond probability. The civil service statute requires that there be geographic representation in hiring but this is not taken seriously. In addition, the percentage of relatives working for the government is extremely high *outside* Washington, far beyond mere chance.

Another important CSRA reform was giving agencies the power to make personnel decisions. Previously, most of this authority was vested in OPM, too much so for efficient management. It was a sound reform, but the Carter OPM policy went too far: 746 agency-examining delegations were made in the two years following the law's enactment. The act required that "common positions" could not be delegated to agencies except under exceptional circumstances. But the Carter OPM delegated all examinations for most occupations between grades GS-9 and GS-15.

In 1981 I became concerned with this mass delegation, given that Congress had explicitly added a common-position exception to the original Carter proposal. On review, my staff found that many of these delegations were neither justifiable on efficiency grounds nor allowable under the law. So I centralized certain authorities to meet legal requirements and to maintain some central integrity in the examination process.

One of the difficulties in making merit work in the merit system was CSRAs expansion of the participation of labor unions in government management decisions. The Carter administration, against its better judgment, was forced to accept this to pass the CSRA. As a result, the federal government system is far more unionized than the private sector, with about 60 percent of employees represented by unions—although only a handful pay dues—compared to under 20 percent of the private sector.

There is a fundamental incompatibility between a civil service system based upon rules and a labor-management system based upon arbitration. A civil service system depends on abstract universal rules, whereas a dispute resolution system of arbitration and grievances rests on individual cases and on circumstances that can be bargained about without much limit from rules. The CSRA created an ambiguous system involving two different employee review tribunals, the Merit System Protection Board and the Federal Labor Relations Authority. On occasion, MSPB and FLRA have decided similar cases but reached inconsistent results. The consequent chaos has been only partially resolved by the courts; sometimes they favor the MSPB rules and sometimes the FLRA's dispute resolution.

In my four years, the unions were very active. Before the CSRA, from 1970 to 1979, 177 cases on negotiability were resolved. During the five succeeding years, the number had exploded to 454 cases. The number of unfair labor practice (ULP) charges soared between fiscal 1980 and 1983 to a total of 21,609.

Of these, 20,653 were filed by the unions. In a 1982 report GAO estimated that the number of ULP charges more than doubled under the CSRA, at a cost in fiscal 1981 alone of $25.9 million.

Union collective bargaining has directly limited the merit aspects of personnel selection in three important ways. It has limited the sources from which candidates for positions can be selected. It has limited whether or not these candidates will be considered simultaneously or sequentially. And it has limited the bases on which relative abilities will be evaluated. Under union-supported "sequential consideration," government management would be required to give first consideration to members of a union bargaining unit before candidates outside the bargaining unit could be considered. Moreover, management would be precluded from expanding the minimum area of consideration to review candidates from other sources, including OPM registers, if a predetermined number of qualified candidates were found in the area of consideration represented by the union. The unions were successful in pressuring the Federal Labor Relations Authority to rule that sequential consideration proposals must be considered as negotiable by management.

Sequential consideration obviously violates merit selection procedures because it gives unit members an advantage over other government employees who do not belong, or those who are outside of government. The merit principle has always been deemed to require selection from the widest possible number of sources. The civil service law requires that "selection and advancement should be determined solely on the basis of relative ability, knowledge, and skill, after fair and open competition which assures that all receive equal opportunity." But under the interpretation of the FLRA—which sees its role as giving labor at least half a loaf—this part of the law is frequently evaded.

Unions also pressured for bargaining over so-called crediting plans, which determine the levels of knowledge, skills, and abilities needed to qualify for a federal job, as well as how these requirements are evaluated. Although in some cases the FLRA has ruled that crediting plans need not be negotiated with unions, in earlier cases it ruled that the procedures were negotiable. Unions also tried to limit management's setting of performance standards by attempting to negotiate work standards and whether managers have to *prove* why they rated in a particular way. To date, even the FLRA has ruled bargaining over critical performance elements nonnegotiable, and the U.S. Court of Appeals for the District of Columbia ruled that management performance decisions are final during the performance appraisal, although it had to overrule FLRA to do so. But the unions keep nibbling away at the merit rules. And who can blame them? Congress created two personnel systems for one work force, with all of the conflicts and irrationality the dual system implies.

The most comprehensive survey of merit violations was the 1982 Merit Systems Protection Board study "Breaking Trust: Prohibited Personnel Practices in the Federal Service." It concluded that "most forms of political abuse— thought to be the greatest threat to the merit system—actually occur at insignificant levels of frequency." The most prevalent abuse— although one would never know it from union complaints or media coverage—was not political manipulation but abuses by career employees through the "buddy system." The buddy system operates, MSPB described, through career employees "granting preferential treatment or access to people known by direct or indirect acquaintance, independent of those persons' merit, relative to other competitors."

Respondents to the MSPB survey were asked whether during the past twelve months they had observed any events that strongly suggested a selection or a job reward based upon something other than merit. Nearly 40 percent of the senior personnel officials reported having seen the buddy system in operation, as did 37 percent of midlevel employees and 29 percent of senior executives. The buddy system works primarily through early knowledge of a job opening, prior knowledge of qualifications, or movement of an individual into a position temporarily to earn needed qualifications. All are widespread practices in the federal personnel system.

The second most prohibited practice observed was discrimination against nonminority males. The study found that 33 percent said they had observed things strongly suggestive of "a person being denied a job or job reward on account of being a non-minority male." Whereas 11 percent said they had observed such behavior toward women because they were women, and 8 percent had witnessed similar discrimination against minority members. Tellingly, blacks reported the same general pattern as did whites.

Although there is widespread belief such merit abuses exist, neither MSPB nor OPM has been able to prove very many. OPM's Agency Compliance and Evaluation unit did find that in 12 percent of the cases it studied, eligible candidates were not listed in proper order. In another 12 percent of their reviews, public notice material did not contain complete job information, and 23 percent of its audits found that public notice in agency recruiting did not result in sufficient eligibles for full certification. In 15 percent of ACE's audits, development of documentation was less than acceptable. In 6 percent of the audits, 10 percent or more of the applications reviewed were not rated correctly. And in 16 percent of ACE's audits, certification files were not documented to provide a clear record of the examination process. Despite this documentation, proof in specific cases has been difficult to obtain. True buddies do not talk.

Merit selection was also complicated by "affirmative action" to give minorities help in examinations not available to nonminorities. In theory, affirmative action should only increase the pool of applicants. In practice, there was preferential treatment, as documented in the MSPB study. The most notorious cases involved selections forced under the PACE "consent decree." Although I fought that decision, both during the transition and into the administration for a full year, I was finally bound by the decree, which said OPM must devise an exam that *guaranteed* that the same proportion of minorities or Hispanics who took any government exam would be selected by it. Of course, this was impossible under a merit exam.

In order to end nonmerit selection in a merit system as soon as possible (since the five years of the decree ran from the date PACE was discontinued), OPM immediately abolished PACE and used "supplemental" examinations. These examinations simply used informal quotas, since that is the only way OPM could comply with the consent decree's required proportions. OPM's decision was the only way out of a very difficult box. Making the decision, I announced to the public that "merit was wounded but not dead." It is still wounded. A new examination was introduced by OPM in 1990, but 50 percent of the score is based upon paper qualifications rather than merit and the other half tends to equalize merit scores.

One modification of the PACE consent decree achieved by the Reagan administration provided that if changes were made in the Uniform Guidelines on Employee Selection, the government could request changes in the decree. The Uniform Guidelines are, on their face, a set of technical requirements for valid examination testing. In fact, they provide the regulatory underpinning for an employee selection system that is outmoded scientifically, inefficient, and overburdensome to any employer, who must prove that he did not discriminate when hiring. Rather than give each party an equal burden of proof, the Uniform Guidelines make the employer prove his innocence, once it is shown that he has hired fewer than the proportion of minorities who happen to live in his metropolitan region. No one can pass this type of rigged test. One of my failures at OPM was in not making much progress in persuading the White House to rewrite these guidelines and end the unequal playing field for employers.

The government could return merit to its personnel examination system by simply returning to the principles that undergirded the original civil service merit system. Open examinations on skill, ability, and knowledge could be given for every job at every level of the government, as required by law. That means so-called career-ladder promotions, which allow individuals to move up grade levels without having to prove the necessary competence, would be eliminated. "Special appointments," except in the area of making reasonable accommodations for disabled individuals, especially veterans, could be eliminated. Nondiscrimination and open access would be guaranteed, and efforts would be made to ensure all segments of the population were aware of the examination, but tests fair to all applicants exist and could be used. In many cases, performance appraisals could be used as an examination to escape the court-created problem of proving that an examination is related to the type of work involved.

To complete the process of creating a fair selection system, the Uniform Guidelines must be revised and the PACE examination sweetheart deal relitigated. This would be especially necessary if the Court extends the five-year coverage period, which appears likely. The Uniform Guidelines assume discrimination simply from the numbers and, therefore, reverse the whole tradition of American law by putting the burden of proof upon the defendant. A recent Supreme Court decision would make change more likely, but Congress is now trying to make the Uniform Guidelines' numbers game the law of the land for all employment decisions.

The easiest way to end the buddy system is to require that the overwhelming proportion of examinations be written. This need not be required at the very highest Senior Executive Service level if written tests or their equivalent were successfully completed at earlier stages. Review boards for senior executives make sense, but for the great majority of civil service positions and promotions, examinations should be written. There is no other way to end the buddy system. In addition, the central personnel agency, OPM, must have enough control to ensure that the giving of examinations is more widely publicized and more widely available to the public.

Is it not ridiculous to have to make a plea for merit in a merit system?

Screening for Employment Suitability

The first letter I received from the chairman of the House civil service subcommittee, right after I became head of the civil service, had a cute little smile drawn within a capital "P" for Patricia Schroeder. Most of the succeeding letters from the congresswoman had a frown.

Schroeder's largest frowns were reserved for my attempts to strengthen national security investigations. OPM has the overall responsibility for conducting background investigations for the civil service, and for setting the rules under which all investigations are made for most who enter the federal service. Before my tenure, self-styled civil libertarians had so weakened the quality of OPM's investigative product and the frequency at which reinvestigations were made that I informed the Reagan transition team that this should be a major item for reform during our administration. From the very beginning, the good congresswoman was concerned that I might reform investigations, and frowned on any such activity by me.

In 1981 Schroeder inserted in the *Congressional Record* a statement expressing an understanding with the chairman of my appropriations subcommittee: if Devine spent funds to investigate the loyalty of employees or applicants for federal employment, he would be in violation of the law. Actually, the law said no such thing and the statement had no binding effect. Pal Patsy was just trying to scare me off. It didn't work.

I searched around for something to keep her busy. In the same initial report, the transition team had found that the cost of one of OPM's executive training centers was substantially higher than the others. Guess where it was located? We investigated and found that the center had actually been moved to Schroeder's district during the Carter administration at a sizable increase in cost. It was difficult to understand why it was moved from California to Denver, except that it might be in the district of the oversight subcommittee chairwoman. One of the budget recommendations of the transition report, therefore, was to consider moving the training center to a more cost-effective location.

Over the next couple of years, I kept the congresswoman occupied responding to rumors that the training center might be moved. How could any congresswoman ignore such nice district pork? We did cost analyses for different cities, which I leaked. Then we began making formal cost-comparison bids. I leaked those too.

She soon called hearings, even one in her Denver district, which she obliged me to attend. We received numerous requests for information, and her chief staffers spent many months trying to thwart us. Unfortunately for them, even the General Accounting Office had to admit that her pork was more expensive than OPM's alternative site and that it made economic sense to move the expensive training center from her district.

For four years, we kept the civil service subcommittee chairwoman and her staff busy while we reformed the background investigation program. Although some form of institutionalized selection and screening process had been in place almost continuously since President Ulysses Grant's Advisory Board of the Civil Service, the program had been badly neglected. After the furor of the McCarthy period in the 1950s, little had been done to implement President Eisenhower's Executive Orders 10450 and 10577. By the time I entered office, the security program under the first executive order and the suitability program under the second had become hopelessly confused.

It is necessary to maintain the distinction between national security considerations and simple suitability for employment because each program has different standards, rights, and legal procedures. To clarify those distinctions, it was necessary to rewrite completely the administrative procedures dealing with the two programs. The suitability program, directly under OPM authority and amendable by internal procedural changes, received the first attention. Suitability simply means that employees must be honest, trustworthy, and otherwise "suitable" for government employment. Without such standards, waste and fraud would cost inordinate sums of money. Even though the number of dishonest government workers is relatively small, a few can do great damage. A GAO study estimated that almost one third of the waste and fraud losses in government traced to dishonest federal workers. Proper suitability programs can limit these losses and promote the efficiency of the service through selection of trustworthy employees.

A suitability program must ensure that candidates have the experience and education they state. The basic suitability program, therefore, checks for counterfeit credentials, falsified résumés, and exaggerated qualifications. Fidelifacts, a New York-based company that checks employee backgrounds, reports that it finds significant derogatory information in 30 percent of its job applicant investigations. Such information generally involves stretching the truth, outright lying, or facts indicating the applicant is unqualified for the position. Similar results have been reported by other companies. The National Credential Verification Service, for example, found that the credentials of seven out of twenty applicants had been falsified. Not surprisingly, federal agencies have experienced similar results. A sample survey of 5,200 investigative reports found that 25 percent had significant derogatory information, and 21 percent had statements or forms falsified. A study of interviews of applicants for employment found falsified data in one fifth of the cases.

Improved suitability procedures in the government resulted in our finding: (a) an "anesthesiologist" employed by an army hospital who had no valid medical degree or license to practice; (b) a contractor working at the Kennedy Space Center who was identified as an escaped convict serving a life sentence for murder; (c) an applicant for a position as a customs inspector who was a member of a cult plotting to use that position as a point of entry for smuggling firearms; (d) an applicant for a position as a prison guard who failed to disclose that his brother was serving a life sentence at the prison; (e) an applicant for a computer programmer position at a nuclear weapons facility which had a capability for automated handling of hot nuclear materials who was a member of a cult demanding total obedience to the cult leader, who opposed related U.S. laws; (f) the wife of an important U.S. nuclear scientist who was carrying on a clandestine affair with a Soviet agent in a European country; (g) a practical nurse at a federal hospital who had a history of repeated prostitution and drug-related offenses over a fifteen-year period; (h) an applicant for a position requiring extensive public contact who had a thirty-year history of stealing, use and sale of narcotics, armed robbery, burglary, possession of heroin, and assault with intent to kill; (i) an applicant for a position in a federal agency responsible for regulating and overseeing the banking industry who had previously been prosecuted for bank fraud and embezzlement of over $500,000; and (j) an applicant for a position of high public trust who had twenty-seven judgments totaling close to $400,000, several bankruptcies, foreclosures, and credit delinquencies.

OPM dramatically improved the quality of suitability investigations performed by the government. But suitability was only part of the problem. One of the most disturbing aspects was that the quality of personnel investigations in the defense area was inferior to the quality of those in the rest of the civil service. When the program was changed in the 1950s, OPM's predecessor agency had delegated authority for investigations in the defense area to the Department of Defense (DOD). By the 1980s, the background investigation for top secret positions conducted by DOD interviewed only half the number of sources that OPM did. Secret clearance was given by the DOD after only a highly inadequate check of records. When I tried to upgrade the investigations, DOD staffers—who have few peers in bureaucratic infighting—leaked to Congress inaccurate information that almost resulted in the removal of DOD from any OPM oversight. In another case, I had to meet personally with Secretary of Defense Caspar Weinberger to overrule lower-level DOD decisions that violated minimal quality requirements for background investigations.

Investigations assistant George Woloshyn and I completely reformulated the investigative product and the mix of different investigations authorized for agencies at various levels of suitability and security clearance. Changes were based upon the best available data, primarily Central Intelligence Agency personnel security surveys. OPM also applied pressure to increase the number of reinvestigations required under OPM guidance, but we achieved only limited success. In one defense agency, OPM found that most components were not complying with periodic reinvestigation requirements at all. They were pressured to change, but the reinvestigations actually undertaken in most agencies did not meet even minimal standards. These agencies fight the OPM program of upgrading reinvestigations to this day. Perhaps that explains why there are so many recent spy scandals.

While we improved the quality of investigations, we also made them less intrusive. In the government, especially in the area of defense, too many positions are classified too highly, resulting in needless and costly investigation. By creating a background investigation product more tailored to specific needs, we were able to reduce the scope of an investigation where appropriate, while intensifying our attention where it was needed at higher levels of trust, or for genuine cases of national security. Finally, OPM set adjudicative standards to cover due process for those who appealed government employment decisions.

One issue left unresolved when I departed was how broadly to use polygraphs. Research data showed that polygraphs had the highest productivity in discovering information that could disqualify for employment. I favored the existing policy of allowing OPM to approve specific cases for polygraph, without making use so broad it would raise civil liberties questions. This system had worked for decades without denying security needs or overly infringing on rights. If the government tightened security procedures as OPM had done for suitability ones, it would not be necessary to overuse polygraphing.

During the debate on the administration proposal to expand the use of polygraphs, an intelligent, extremely left-wing aide to Congresswoman Schroeder, Andy Feinstein—once, when pressed at a hearing for a definition of "liberal,"

I had pointed at him—went to Fort McClellan, Alabama, to learn how the Department of Defense trains polygraph examiners. His hidden purpose was to expose the polygraph's defects. As Feinstein was strapped into the polygraph device, the examiner told him the questions in advance and the staffer bluffed his way through the tricky ones, lying on purpose to see how the machine would react.

As the test was ending, the examiner threw in an unexpected question, asking if Feinstein had played a role in defeating my renomination for a second term as director of OPM, after he had publicly denied doing so. The polygraph tester reported that, without speaking, the smart staffer "answered" the question with a series of widely erratic lines at the right end of the polygraph paper. The polygraph said "yes" by measuring increases in blood pressure, respiration, and perspiration. The left-wing staffer got a good lesson in the accuracy of the polygraph.

In spite of determined opposition, we were able to implement higher standards for suitability and we had begun the process of reforming national security investigations. The president had ordered that the director of OPM work with the attorney general to reform national security investigations. Progress was delayed for a year by the political gamesmanship over the nomination of Edwin Meese as attorney general. By the time that was resolved, my time in the barrel had started, and I was soon to depart. But while I was there, we were able completely to reform the background investigations program, generating more pertinent information, even while providing more protection for civil liberties, and all at a lower cost—a process insiders tell me continues. But there were no more smiles on my letters.

Making a Federal Case over Charity

From its beginnings under President Eisenhower and its incorporation in a regulation under an executive order issued by President Kennedy, the government's Combined Federal Campaign (CFC) charitable drive was limited to traditional health and welfare charitable organizations. For almost thirty years, the CFC was conducted by and with those traditional charities. Late in the Carter administration, however, certain legal defense and other political advocacy groups sued to be admitted into the CFC. Their argument was that the CFC was an open government forum and that to prevent any group from soliciting funds in that forum was to restrict their freedom of speech. The first suit was won on a technicality by the political advocacy groups, and they were admitted into the CFC during the preceding administration.

When I first reviewed this issue, I was amazed. The criteria for admittance into the CFC and the way funds were distributed were completely arbitrary. So we reformed them. But I thought it was preposterous that political advocacy groups should be able to join a charitable drive. A charitable drive, it seemed to me, was a time when the disparate elements of a community united to focus upon what all considered good, charitable works. To allow political groups to enter the campaign was to destroy that consensus necessary to a combined charitable drive. Besides, it violated logic. Charity should be limited to charitable organizations.

When we made the reforms and included only the traditional charities in the CFC, we were enjoined from enforcing them. We had to make a federal case out of the matter and appeal to the Supreme Court to achieve what seemed to be common sense. Unfortunately for us, many of the new advocacy groups were legal defense funds that existed to sue other people. They certainly justified their existence in the CFC cases. We were in court more than twenty times over three years before we won a four-to-three Supreme Court decision that said we had the right to limit the charity to charitable organizations.

My concern that a charity needed a consensus across a wide spectrum of groups was confirmed the first full year we ran the CFC with political groups. The preceding year, only the leftist groups which had sued were engaged in the charitable drive, and there was little problem. But if you admit left-wing political groups, you must admit the right too. The tolerance of the pro-abortionists was strained when the National Right to Life Committee entered the campaign. Then the unions became upset when the National Right to Work Legal Defense and Education Fund was admitted. As a result, in several communities the unions boycotted the CFC charitable drive. Soon everyone was at each other's throat over sweet charity. The result of the politicization: 500,000 fewer employees participated in the charity drive.

To prevent a repeat the following year, I drafted a new executive order from President Reagan to govern the campaign operations. Designed to concentrate CFC's limited resources in the most essential philanthropic activities and to restore contributors' faith in the campaign, the new rules would formally limit CFC participation to traditional health and welfare charitable organizations.

As the Reagan order was being tested in the courts, the administration received editorial support from both the *Wall Street Journal* and the *Washington Post*. The *Post* concluded thus: the "Federal government, through the CFC, should not be a collection agency for clearly political groups. That kind of open 'charity' begins at home or someplace else." Unfortunately, the White House, the Department of Justice, and the counsel of OMB were not so enthusiastic. We were forced to modify the regulations to allow some political advocacy. But, at least, we did put some limits upon the types of groups that could be admitted to a charity campaign.

Finally, the Supreme Court ruled. Reagan appointee Sandra Day O'Connor wrote for the Court that "the government does not violate the First Amendment when it limits participation in order to minimize disruption to the federal work place, to ensure the success of the fundraising effort, or to avoid the appearance of political favoritism." She said that President Reagan "could reasonably conclude that a dollar spent directly providing food or shelter to the needy is more beneficial than a dollar spent on litigation that might or might not result in aid to the needy." Thank heaven, the courts had finally ruled for common sense. Even so, the legal defense funds pledged further legal action, and the challenge in the courts continues to this day. I guess that is how they make their living, but it seems not very charitable.

9

Reforming the Buddy System

Good Pay and Benefits

Would you like a job with pleasant working conditions, lifetime employment, competitive wages, and great promotion potential? One that also happens to pay you double the national average pension after thirty years of work? You can retire at age fifty-five—ten years before most of your peers will receive benefits—and you are still young enough to obtain another job. While you work at your new job, your retirement benefits from the old one will be paid at a rate indexed to the full degree of inflation, guaranteeing your earning power for the rest of your life.

Had the above been written several years ago, not only would you have received full indexing of the total benefits you would still receive—virtually unknown in any other job—but you would have got the compounding effects of having it paid twice yearly. You would also have been able to "look back" to get the previous year's cost-of-living increase too. Indeed, because you were so valued, you would have received a 1 percent "kicker" cost-of-living increase on top of that. Now, that's cost-of-living protection with a vengeance! Sound good? Well, then, you should have signed up for federal government employment. Unfortunately, because the deal was so sweet, ten people were waiting ahead of you for every job—twenty at the higher-paid levels.

Still, the official government survey contended that federal employee salaries were 20 percent below those in the private sector. There are *also* government studies that show that federal employees are paid 11 percent more than private sector employees—but these are kept quiet. One needs no formal study to guess which of these studies is correct when ten are waiting for every opening.

While I was at OPM the government once announced a few dozen blue collar federal jobs openings in a southern city. Three thousand people lined up for them. After the riot, even I had to agree that the agency should keep future openings more quiet. Janitors in the government earn $4,000 more than those in the private sector, and when openings are advertised, attract thousands of highly educated teachers. As for shipbuilding workers, I was told by private sector executives that they do not even try to compete with the government. They just wait for the feds to retire and then hire them for the last decade of their work life, a decade handsomely enriched by those federal pensions. Given this, are you now convinced which study is correct?

When considering pay, retirement, and other benefits, one must conclude that federal workers as a group are well ahead of most similarly skilled workers in the private sector. Some are not paid enough. We pay the hard workers the same as those who goof off. We spend a hugh amount on deferred benefits like pensions, which most employees will not receive, and do not pay enough up front in salary to the majority.

OPM undertook a comprehensive analysis of the government's pay study, and the analysis was confirmed by two outside studies (although both modified their language so they might get future contracts from the government). The basic problem with the original survey was pretty easy to spot. As a professor, I had taught survey methodology. The survey used by the government to measure pay was more flawed than the one I had used in school to illustrate a biased survey. The Bureau of Labor Statistics performed the actual survey rather competently although there were some technical problems. It was the design of the sample, however, that was most biased, and this was created by a government board which included federal sector union members. The survey was biased toward high-paying jobs in the private sector and low-paying jobs in the government, to make the federal government look as if it were paying less than did the private sector.

Specifically, a large sample was drawn for professional jobs where the private sector often paid more. For administrative jobs, which represent a very high proportion of federal jobs, a minuscule sample was drawn. Large samples were selected from the private sector from high-paying manufacturing positions, and few from lower-paying service industries. The survey oversampled high-paying large corporations from the private sector and hardly sampled from companies with fewer than fifty employees, although the law required that the entire "private sector" be sampled, not a portion of it. Companies with fifty or fewer employees provide the vast majority of jobs in the nation. State and local governments—the most comparable jobs to those in the federal government—were not allowed to be placed in the survey. May one suspect that this was because state and local government employees are paid less than those in the federal government? Moreover, when specific jobs were matched in the private and public sectors, the benefit of the doubt was always given to what would result in higher wages in the private sector, justifying more pay for federal employees.

When OPM made a correction for these errors and the others it found, the average federal employee was paid 4 percent more than his equivalent in the private sector. Our overall estimate, based upon census figures, was that the federal government paid 11 percent more. But the gap differed by income levels. Both low- and high-grade positions were underpaid, whereas the vast majority of jobs in the middle were *much* overpaid. When we made these results available to an association representing federal managers, results showing that they were the group most underpaid, they were not especially interested in our study. They wanted to preserve the myth that all federal employees were underpaid—and not threaten their coalition with the unions on pay and benefits questions—rather than represent their own clients who in fact were underpaid.

When these figures were made public, federal employees were outraged. And low-graded employees did not make their own case any more than did top managers. All chose to stand together and ignore the data. When the president determined that federal wages should be cut in his 1985 budget, I presented our data as justification for such a cut in what the *Wall Street Journal* correctly labeled "counter-gamesmanship" because I additionally suggested that the only alternative to a pay decrease was to cut a hundred thousand jobs. Although the federal community said it was unimpressed, when it was confronted with the possibility of job loss, the opposition to the president's proposal cooled noticeably. Even my suggestion in the same study to compute federal pay under market methods received a decent hearing when compared to my idea of cutting jobs.

At this juncture, Congresswoman Mary Rose Oakar (D-Ohio) came up with a marvelous plan to correct federal pay inequities: "comparable worth." Her idea was to pay federal employees what a government official decides a job is "worth" to society compared with all other jobs. This is how it would be calculated: nurses and doctors perform indispensable services, and since a rating scheme can be devised to prove that both are equally worthwhile, nurses should be paid the same as doctors. The only reason doctors and nurses are not paid equally is that nursing is a predominantly female occupation, and doctoring is predominantly a male one. This "discrimination" should be ended by government surveys that measure the true societal worth of jobs, so all may be paid "fairly."

That in a nutshell is "comparable worth". To measure these jobs, Oakar proposed a modified version of the standard job evaluation device measuring clerical positions. This device was viewed as neutral and "scientific." The only problem was that it was designed to measure white collar work, not blue collar work. Using it to measure blue collar work is like using a yardstick to measure temperature.

OPM performed a study to gauge the effects of using the comparable-worth methodology to rate government jobs. We had an especially large data base in the government's Central Personnel Data File, which includes all federal employees. We came up with a large sample of 8,500 employees, a sampling that would give us great statistical reliability. We used linear multiple-regression techniques on all the background variables available in our large file. Our explanatory model predicted over 75 percent of the variance in why people are paid differently, making it a reliable explanation.

The study showed that differences in federal employee salaries are explainable by rational, achievement-oriented decisions. Receiving a college degree and adding experience to it led to the highest salary. The willingness to accept supervisory responsibility gave the next highest return in income. Then came experience, location and willingness to relocate, early educational choices of career fields with the highest potential payoff, and the amount of time one is willing to invest in work. Sexual discrimination explained only 1.3 percent of the variance. Choice of occupation was a critical factor, but, contrary to the expectation of comparable-worth theories, if a man chose a clerical occupation, it cost him more income than a woman. It is not sexual discrimination that leads to lower pay for clerical occupations, because men receive a greater penalty than women for choosing that occupation. It is simply a matter of choice.

Having pay set arbitrarily by government evaluation studies and not determined by market demand leads to what Hank Cox called a "pay police" system, which would be necessary to enforce the millions of pay decisions made every day. The freedom to bargain for wages would be taken from employees and their representative unions if pay were to be set under comparable worth. Likewise, no job evaluation system can work unless it adjusts for market forces, without being extremely arbitrary. As Chief Justice Weiner of the U.S. District Court in Colorado said, in a decision against comparable worth, such a system would create "absolute chaos in the economy" and is "pregnant with the possibility of disrupting the entire economic system in the United States."

Choice of any single system to evaluate every job is too rigid to meet real-world realities. Using a white collar system to measure blue collar work clearly is harmful and unfair to those in blue collar work. At OPM, we used the government's white collar system to classify blue collar jobs to show what the effect would be. If the white collar system were used, both custodial male workers and laundry female workers would be cut from a $16,000 blue collar salary to one of $10,000 measured by clerical worth. Women in food service and male laborers would both receive a $5,000 wage cut relative to clerk-typist women. Female store workers and male forklift operators would receive at least $4,000 less relative to that got by female nursing assistants. Female sewing machine operators and male warehouse workers would receive about $3,000 less compared to salaries for women secretaries. And this continued on across each grade level as different classes and sexes were advantaged or disadvantaged by the arbitrary classification scheme.

Is it arbitrary or fair to pay a worker in a sooty factory the same as a nursing assistant in a hygienic hospital? Should a staffing specialist in an office be paid the same as a boiler plant operator? Should a pipe operator be paid the same as an accounting technician? Should explosives operators be paid the same as a clerk-typist? What a tangle of value questions comparable worth would create!

Comparable worth simply is a recipe for conflict. And it would be conflict not between the sexes, but between the classes. Blue collar men and women would be disadvantaged relative to both white collar men and women. Naturally, the blue collar workers would resent this unfairness and rise against it.

Where were the protectors of the blue collar working class, the industrial labor unions? Well, with one honorable exception—the Marine Engineers Beneficial Association—the unions made a cynical decision not to oppose comparable worth. Since they could not further organize within the blue collar community, they would use comparable worth as an organizing device for white collar workers, a predominantly female labor force they think can be conned by comparable-worth scare tactics. Somehow I think women will not let them succeed.

The Retirement System

Let us return to the existing system. So far, we have discussed federal compensation without pensions. The generosity of the federal retirement system defies description to average Americans. With a preretirement salary of $25,000, a federal employee will receive at least $200,000 *more* over a twenty-year period than a person with the same preretirement salary in the private sector. With a $50,000 preretirement salary, a federal manager will receive $1 million more than his private sector counterpart. No wonder federal employees retire as close to age fifty-five as they are able to retire and receive full benefits. Median retirement age in the federal government is sixty for normal retirements, compared with sixty-five in the private sector.

Not only are there large inequities between the public and private sector, but some federal employees are treated far better than others. Almost 40 percent of federal employees receive little or nothing from retirement benefits, sometimes even subsidizing the pension system for the benefit of their longer-staying associates. Only those who stay a full career in the government get the full benefit. These retire after thirty years and collect fully indexed benefits for the rest of their lives. Most federal employees serve for a few years and then leave for the private sector. But the relatively few who serve a full career do extremely well.

These few cost the nation dearly. The Civil Service Retirement System was the government's third-largest entitlement program. Over $20 billion per year went to about a million people. Besides this direct cost to the taxpayer, there was an incomprehensible, unfunded liability of over half a trillion dollars in 1984. This is an obligation for every taxpayer in the United States and will be paid in the future unless something is done to bring this extremely costly system under control. Although much attention has been focused on the social security system's problems over the last few years, the federal pension system has been *far more* out of control. While social security outlays increased by 1,209 percent between 1960 and 1980, government contributions to the Civil Service Retirement System grew 2,351 percent.

When the Reagan administration proposed reforms in this area, federal employees and retirees were incensed by this "breach of contract." But most of the expensive CSRS benefits were put into effect during the service of most current federal retirees, not when they were hired. Several times while I was director of OPM, I offered to return to all federal employees' original contracts, when they were hired, and to propose no other changes to the retirement system. I was never taken up on the challenge.

The reforms that the Reagan administration did propose made common sense. We proposed to move the normal retirement age from fifty-five to the private sector's norm of age sixty-five (actually, we kept the retirement age the same, but assessed the full actuarial penalty used in the private sector for early retirement before age sixty-five). And we proposed to put a lid on the percentage that the cost-of-living adjustment could increase each year, to raise employee contributions to the point that they would equal the government contribution, and to make the total benefit formula comparable to those in the private sector. Employees over the age of fifty-five were exempted from any changes, and the effects of the other changes were phased in. We did save about $2 billion legislatively, and made other changes administratively that saved about $10 billion. This is progress, but the other reforms need to be adopted to normalize federal compensation.

Since the government has extremely low turnover relative to the private sector, this "holding power" of federal compensation policy costs taxpayers billions of dollars in inflated personnel costs each year. Several OPM studies have verified this, and a recent paper presented by Dartmouth professor Steven Venti at a Bureau of Economic Research conference estimates that federal employee compensation was between 16 and 42 percent higher than necessary relative to market factors.

Government employees, however, never cease "proving" they are underpaid—especially at the General Accounting Office, the principal ombudsman for federal employee compensation. GAO has plenty of experience in manipulating statistics. For example, instead of using the turnover, "quit rates" used in private personnel management, government statisticians produce what they call staffing "turbulence" data. These statistics show that a large number of government employees transfer between assignments within the federal government. Of course, the solution to this problem, if it is a problem, is to end or modify automatic reassignment rights, which have nothing to do with basic turnover for pay or benefits.

The other favorite of GAO is to focus upon the large number of federal employees who transfer between various agencies of the government. Of course, this has nothing to do with general conditions of employment for the federal government such as pay or government benefits, since most agencies have basically the same pay and benefits, but it does have to do with other government policies that encourage transfers between departments. If transfers are the problem, they can be limited.

The only relevant fact for turnover is how many people leave the government. And the figures here are uncookable: the overall turnover rate for the private sector ranges between 10 and 25 percent, whereas for government employees it has never been above 7 percent. The only remotely comparable private sector industry, communications, was until recently so regulated that it must be considered quasi-governmental. Here, on the average, less than half as many employees turn over from federal government sinecures as change jobs in the private sector.

The causes are not difficult to ascertain. In the first few years of employment, turnover among federal bureaucrats is only a bit lower than that for their brethren in the private sector. As they get closer to vesting in the government's extremely generous retirement system, turnover rates drop sharply. After the five years it takes to become vested for retirement benefits, turnover drops from 10 to 5 percent and then declines quickly to below 3 percent.

Tenure in government positions is much higher than that in the private sector, for one simple reason: a highly attractive retirement benefits system gives strong incentives for long-term employment. The extreme stability in government employment not only costs billions of dollars but, as important, also crushes vitality within the bureaucracy.

The tragedy is that this system can be reformed in the public interest, with federal employees' own long-term interests not compromised. We merely need to pay at market rates and create a retirement system with reasonable benefits, broadly shared, *but a system which also allows the pension benefits to be retained if one leaves employment*. As director of OPM I made a proposal that would have made benefits fully portable, thus solving that part of the problem. Several employee association group representatives expressed support for my fully portable retirement system, and the *Washington Post*'s "Federal-Beat" columnist Mike Causey found sizable support for the idea among his readers. But the bureaucrats at OMB defeated the idea. The retirement system adopted for new federal employees after I left did make benefits somewhat more portable, a modest step in the right direction.

There is nothing that will kill employee morale more than tying a person to a job for thirty years. That has been the policy of the federal government. Many employees in the federal government, with as little as five or ten years of service, feel trapped for the next two decades of their lives, until they can receive their retirement checks. This breeds boredom, resentment, and inefficiency. Our retirement system benefits no one, not even federal employees. But the retirement system dominated the thinking of federal employees during my tenure as civil service chief. Pensions were to be protected, without any change, whatever the cost. And, except for employees hired after the Reagan social-security reforms put new federal employees under social security, little has changed for most federal employees.

Federal government workers often express wonder why proposals are put forth each year to restructure their retirement system. Even with the wicked old "Grinch of the Civil Service" gone, similar proposals appear in the president's budget each year. Federal employees must recognize that private sector employees (which means most Americans) cannot understand why federal employees should be such a richly rewarded class. Until federal employees decide to get behind some serious proposals for overall pay and benefit reforms, these assaults will continue, Grinch or no Grinch.

Making the Market Work for Health Benefits

My most radical success at OPM was the complete restructuring of a major government program, which saved billions of dollars for taxpayers, and even financially benefited employees. Yet the only reason I was successful with this program was that I could do it administratively, without needing Congress to change the law. It happened early enough in my tenure that Congress did not believe I had the nerve to make such major reforms without requesting a change in the law. And they—as in most program areas—did not know how the program worked, so were reluctant to offer alternatives that might make the crisis worse and result in criticism for them. The program was the Federal Employee Health Benefits program, a $6 billion-a-year operation that provided health insurance coverage for ten million federal employees, retirees, and their families. It is the fifteenth-largest entitlement program in the government.

Public and private spending on health care and health insurance had exploded, growing much more rapidly than the economy. The numbers were startling. Total national health care spending increased approximately 600 percent between 1967 and 1982, rising from about $50 billion to over $300 billion. In 1982, even with general inflation under control, health care costs rose 11.9 percent, more than three times the cost-of-living increase of 3.9 percent. Cost increases were particularly great in hospital service and in high-tech areas. The average hospitalization cost in constant dollars increased from $22 per day in 1955 to more than $100 per day in 1981—$337 a day in current dollars. More important, out-of-pocket expenses for patients decreased from 30 percent to 11 percent of the average hospital bill, with third-party payers such as insurance companies picking up the difference.

I felt we needed to make employees and retirees aware of the costs of health care and insurance in their economic decisionmaking as they chose health insurance plans. Moreover, since many of the plans under the FEHB system provided first-dollar coverage for hospital stays, the real costs of health care were hidden from the employee.

Not only were there problems in the health and insurance industry generally, past mismanagement of the FEHB exacerbated our situation. In election years, political considerations led to substantial increases in health insurance benefits without setting rates high enough to offset these costs. Instead, while premiums were held to artificially low levels, reserve margins providing protection against unforeseen losses were shaved. The net income to FEHB's trust fund, as a result of this and other imprudent decisions, dropped from an excess over claims of $232 million in fiscal year 1978 to a deficit of $442 million in fiscal year 1981. Since no attention had been given to costs, utilization by employees rose sharply, thereby increasing costs for agencies, employees, retirees, and taxpayers. Not even a workable internal-control system existed at OPM to give warning of the impending cost overrun in 1981.

To avoid a $440 million cost overrun in 1981 and a one-quarter percent average increase in premiums paid by employees and retirees, I ordered two rounds of reforms to FEHB benefits during contract negotiations in the fall of 1981. Reductions in cost were achieved by introducing or expanding cost-sharing features like deductibles and coinsurance in the various health plans in the system, numbering several hundred overall. By introducing deductibles and coinsurance features, employees and retirees were forced to accept cost sharing and its consequent economies. This was especially so in the area of in-hospital deduction and coinsurance, which did not exist or existed at very low levels in the plans with the largest enrollment. Just a few months after these decisions were made, a Rand study found that deductibles and coinsurance were effective in reducing utilization and cost, without significant reduction in the quality of health care.

Not only did these reforms save billions of dollars for taxpayers, but employees benefited too. One million employees switched plans during the annual season when they are allowed to do so, saving themselves billions in otherwise higher premiums. Several plans owned by unions were at the point of bankruptcy. In private discussions afterward, they thanked me for saving their health benefits systems for their members.

Publicly? That was a different matter. In 1981, the unions mounted a large-scale reaction to my reforms, arguing that I would destroy FEHB, changing it from a guaranteed benefits program to an insurance plan. Congress and the media swelled the chorus. OPM endured a score of lawsuits over whether I had the authority to make the changes administratively. After losing all of these cases at the district court level, we prevailed on all fronts at the court of appeals—the only one we lost was over my plan to eliminate coverage of abortions under FEHB. Even there, I was able to jawbone companies representing 80 percent of enrollees to eliminate these benefits "freely," and eventually was successful in pushing Congress to adopt the Ashbrook-Smith amendment, which completely eliminated abortions under the FEHB program.

This was a program area where the government led the private sector. Our reforms were made in 1981. In 1982 a *New York Times* public opinion poll showed that a majority of Americans said they would be willing to accept less expensive policies which did not provide full coverage in order to keep down costs. Between 1981 and 1983 a survey of 1,400 large private sector corporations, by the William H. Mercer Company, found that 468 companies modified their health insurance programs to require employees to pay a higher percentage of the premium, or to increase coinsurance. Seventy percent of the employers were found to be considering such cost sharing in the future. State legislatures followed by acting upon more than three hundred pieces of health care cost-containment legislation in 1984, and were considering four hundred additional pieces in 1985. Fourteen states specifically went to direct cost sharing, including Maryland, which announced an increase of 50 percent in the employee contribution to insurance costs and a doubling of the deductible amount.

Not surprisingly, for the first time since such statistics were collected, hospital admissions began falling in 1985 and costs began a much lower rate of increase. In the FEHB plan itself billions of dollars were saved. For once, the federal government had led the private sector in the adoption of a management efficiency reform. But the federal establishment did not like it one bit. Many, including most congressmen and their spouses, thought I had ruined their FEHB by turning it from a welfare plan to a true insurance program.

Fighting Parkinson's Law

The principal job the president asked me to accomplish was to help him reduce federal nondefense government employment. In doing this, however, we were fighting one of the few immutable "laws" of political science, Professor C. Northcote Parkinson's classic, "bureaucracies grow."

Since the dawn of government, bureaucrats have justified their jobs by hiring people to help them. This meant that the bureaucrat did not have to work as hard and got paid more, and also that bossing subordinates made him look so important that no one thought of getting rid of his job. The only way bureaucracies got reformed was when barbarians took them apart brick by brick and head by head.

My job was to be a modern barbarian, to implement the president's campaign pledge to the people to cut nondefense bureaucracy. The president's first act was to send the message to the bureaucracy that he was not kidding. Instead of adopting the half measures of his predecessor, he slapped a total freeze on new hiring. President Reagan then set goals to reduce the size of nondefense employment and left the mechanics to his management team.

I first briefed the cabinet and other top management officials in the agencies on a proposal to reduce employment primarily through attrition, rather than firings, to provide the most humane, as well as the most cost-efficient, policy. In late December 1981 OPM's informal earlier guidance was codified, citing the various tools available for reducing employment while operating within lower agency budgets. Stressing actions to achieve reductions through attrition, the document also described the responsibilities and rights necessary when attrition would not solve the problem, including using reductions in force (RIFs), furloughs, and increased placement activities.

The *New York Times* noted that 1981 had seen the first reduction in total government employment since just after World War II, and only the fourth decline since World War I. Equally important, the *Times* remarked that both government officials and public employee union leaders agreed that "the years of growth (in government employment) are over." According to OPM figures, the Reagan administration reduced federal employment by 52,983 between the inauguration and the end of 1981. By the end of 1982 we had reduced nondefense civilian work force employment by 113,105 employees, the largest since Dwight D. Eisenhower's tenure. However, unlike those of the Eisenhower administration, the reductions were achieved primarily through attrition. Indeed, government statistics show that over 90 percent of the Reagan administration personnel reductions were achieved through attrition, at a much lower cost than RIFs. In addition, almost thirty thousand employees were relocated to different positions to utilize skills where needed and to save jobs.

The independent Merit Systems Protection Board, in a comprehensive survey of the actions taken by OPM, stated that the administration reduced the human costs of RIFs, finding that over 99 percent of the permanent employees were not affected at all by RIFs. Career specialists in personnel management said that the administration's attrition policy reduced the impact of RIFs, 86 percent saying that it was effective in reducing the possibility of a RIF in their agency. Most noteworthy, 83 percent of employees did not find that performance appraisals were manipulated to affect RIF results. Only 2 percent said that RIFs were not conducted fully in accordance with regulations.

The study found that morale was adversely affected by the RIFs. Yet 64 percent of those in an agency affected by a RIF (but only 30 percent of those in agencies without RIFs) said that lower morale did not result in an equivalent decrease in productivity. Only 13 percent of the employees in RIF-affected agencies said that the quality of work they did actually suffered. Only one quarter said that the quantity of their work was affected at all, and 9 percent said that only their time or attendance at work was affected. Clearly, we had taken a successful stab at Parkinson's law by reducing numbers, in the most humane manner for our employees, without reducing the quality of work. In fact, the tension introduced into the system probably improved productivity.

After 1982 I decided to take on Parkinson's law more directly. But it took me months before I could get my bureaucrats at OPM to admit even that the "Supervisory Grade Evaluation Standard" existed. It was hidden in a multivolume set of looseleaf sheets, written in nearly unintelligible language. It works like this. There are eighteen classified grades (modified today at the top with the Senior Executive Service) where the work of a job is classified according to its duties, and paid more as one moves upward. One advances by having supervisory or managerial duties. Naturally, the rules say this should not determine higher salaries, but in fact it does. To supervise, one must oversee at least three individuals. The trick to rising through our bureaucracy is to find these three, and you are on your way to the top.

I began a series of reforms aimed at getting to the root of all those incentives that encouraged growth. OPM backed an experiment on the West Coast to simplify the government's ponderous multilevel classification system to a five-level system. The experiments showed that it could work and save money. It would also mean fewer classifiers and personnel clerks to create unnecessary position descriptions and other paperwork, which would save the taxpayer more millions of dollars. The simplified system would be a pure pay-for-performance system. A basic rate high enough to attract quality individuals would be set by Congress, the president, and the central management agencies, but within that general guideline and between only five grade levels, all pay would be based on performance. We attacked the overstaffing in the midlevels of the federal government through our so-called bulge-reduction project, targeting elimination of whole levels of duplication of effort.

OPM also began work to revise the Supervisory Standard itself. One proposal would loosen the rigid rule-of-three requirement and install rather a more flexible system to organize government for work, than one organized around arbitrary rules. OPM adopted other reforms too. We tried to contract out to the private sector the government's expensive training function. In true bureaucratic form, OPM career executives fought this all the way. To them, it was a question of saving jobs for fellow government employees. Actually, it gave OPM's central training staff new status. By managing the new contracting process, OPM not only could improve training, but also would assume the more important role of quality control for all government training.

Work-force management policy was also modified to obtain a better balance between permanent government employees and temporary employees. As a result of the 1981 reductions in force, more temporary employees were separated than permanent employees. This was precisely how such a policy should work, but by 1984 the government had too many permanent employees relative to temporary ones. This not only unnecessarily increased costs, but also strangled the infusion of new ideas and energy into the work force. Indeed, for a long period of time, the government had neglected and even discouraged the use of temporary employees through its regulations.

I amended the civil service rules to allow agencies greater discretion in hiring and retaining temporary employees. Immediately, I was attacked by the unions for subverting the professional status of the civil service. By supporting temporaries I must be demeaning permanent employees. Of course, I was implementing what many private sector planners called "core and rim" work-force planning. Under this, there is a central core of long-term employees, with a rim of temporary employees who enter and leave the organization. It saves money and provides for more efficient service. Although I received widespread praise from private sector executives on making the employment mix more flexible, the Washington news media chose to emphasize the union attacks. They had to sell newspapers. I had to try to manage the government efficiently. Fortunately, my policy worked. Temporary employment grew 30 percent the first year of the new program.

The Reagan administration did take some effective steps to fight Parkinson's law. But inefficiencies remained rampant. The President's Private Sector Survey on Cost Control (the Grace commission) worked for eighteen months and made twenty-five hundred recommendations to save hundreds of billions of dollars. It found the largest achievable reforms were in the area of personnel management. The proposals OPM made to Congress to reform personnel, many of which appeared in the Grace commission report, would have saved $60 billion over five years. OPM adopted as many administratively as was possible during my tenure, but many remained out in the cold. *If these reforms were all adopted, the federal deficit could largely be eliminated by personnel reforms alone!* That is how important it is to make personnel management work the way the textbooks say it should, or at least in some rough Washington approximation.

III

Doing It Right

10

Zero Option for the White House

Now let us turn to the solutions to controlling government bureaucracy, starting at the top—the White House. My conclusion, after four years of close observation in the government and three decades of study, is stark but simple: the president could better manage the executive branch if he abolished the White House Office and the Executive Office of the President. Why? Both management theory and practice say that executive responsibility should be given to the line officers who are accountable for getting the job done, and not to staff who tend to create inefficiencies, empires, and paperwork.

There was no White House staff to speak of until relatively recently. George Washington had only his nephew, who volunteered his services. Indeed, it was not until President Buchanan, just before the Civil War, that there was any paid staff for the White House at all. It is perhaps difficult to believe, but there was no institutionalized presidency until

1921, when the Budget and Accounting Act was passed. Even by 1939 with the creation of the Executive Office of the President, there were only six administrative assistants for the White House Office.

In 1937 a total of 37 staffers manned the White House Office, by 1954 there were 266, and by 1971 over 600 were employed. Today, we cannot even count the several thousands in the Executive Office, since many are on detail or otherwise assigned to the White House without appearing on its records. But, I assure you, they are there. The question is, Why did Ronald Reagan require one hundred times the staff that Franklin Roosevelt—fighting the Great Depression and World War II—needed?

A similar staff explosion has taken place in the private sector, and the number of layers between the operating individual and the top of the organization has mushroomed. But the federal government has 50 percent more personnel in midlevel positions than the average business in the private sector and it has many more layers. Moreover, the private sector is beginning to do something about this problem following the lessons taught by Drucker, and Peters and Waterman. We even made a beginning in the bowels of the federal bureaucracy, with my bulge-reduction project, but we did nothing at the top corporate level in the White House.

The real problem with bloated staff is not primarily that it costs a lot (although billions of unnecessary dollars are involved), but that staffers get in the way, and do not allow the line operating officers to carry out their missions, at least not efficiently. Staff reports turn top management attention from the real problems of production to peripheral ones like production numbers.

The basic task facing any business is to get the mission accomplished efficiently, to get the right people to do the right job in the most efficient manner. It is not necessary or appropriate to eliminate staff completely, but top management must discipline itself to focus upon the job to be done. For example, the Japanese "just-in-time" delivery of materials to the manufacturing production line saves inventory costs. But the *major* benefit is to force a discipline upon the whole manufacturing process. It forces management attention on the real problem, which is to perform the mission by increasing production and productivity, rather than wasting time coordinating inventory staff with production employees.

Rather than do the difficult management job from the president through the cabinet to the rest of the government, the recent approach has been to assume that all can be done "within the presidency." That is, by the policy and budget staffs in the White House and the Office of Management and Budget (OMB). Compared to making cabinet government work, the Wilsonian theory deemed it more proper and easier to create a large staff, presumably loyal to the president, which rules by force: threatening on budgets, or regulations, or policy memoranda, or perks, or press leaks.

Force simply does not work. I never had much trouble getting around OMB or the White House Office, because *as a line manager I had the legal authority*. Other agency heads may have been more cautious but were no less able to avoid the White House police. The problem was the delay the staff caused.

When I was waiting to get the regulations approved by OMB to reform our charitable drive, I was facing a tough congressional hearing where Barney Frank (D-Mass.)—the head of the Americans for Democratic Action—was demanding my head for excluding his left-wing friends. In desperation, I was forced to invoke a clause in the OMB powers that said an agency could proceed with regulations after a period of days if OMB had not acted. Although I was the only one who used this loophole (OMB closed it afterward), everyone knew the less extreme tricks.

My deputy—who inherited my job after I was denied reconfirmation—learned this from me too well. She saw that the agency head with the legal authority has the power, not the White House staff, and tested the limits of that power after my term expired. She frustrated what the president actually wanted for the charity drive by bluntly refusing to cooperate and, then, she fired my former aides against direct White House orders. It took the White House more than six months of trying different ways to force her to resign, making the White House staff and the president look ridiculous by prolonging the process: a case study in poor personnel management.

The centralized presidency has been crushed under the weight of the responsibilities given to the national government in the twentieth century. Centralization becomes more and more difficult as the number and complexity of tasks are increased. As F. A. Hayek has shown, decisionmaking must be decentralized so people near the decision with the necessary detailed information can make rational decisions. So, as society becomes more complex, the need for many more and smaller governments grows, and justifies under management principles the usefulness of defederalization as a means to shed national functions. But even a much smaller national government could not be managed the way Woodrow Wilson suggested.

The challenge facing every top executive is to define his situation and then act to achieve his mission. To do this, he needs information and communication of that information from others, since no one can know everything. As Ludwig von Mises has demonstrated, an individual's ability to absorb the necessary information within an organization is finite. When decisions must be made at the top of a large organization, the major problem becomes how to communicate the necessary information to the top. Getting a message to a president is so difficult that we pay some of the highest salaries in the nation to lobbyists who are able to get the information where it is desired. But still the president can receive only so much information. A nation of skilled lobbyists would overwhelm the system.

The Wilsonian response to this problem was to create staff to process information for the top executive. But as government grew and Congress created more and more line agencies, the White House staff kept growing to keep up with more and larger agencies. The line organization already is a communications network that decentralizes decisionmaking, and the addition of staff simply creates more links in the communications network, making understanding and action even more difficult.

The White House Office and OMB are an excuse not to deal with this complex communications apparatus of the national government. A piece of paper in a file somewhere, written by a presumably loyal presidential agent, becomes a substitute for the complex communication process necessary to develop a decision that truly expresses the chief executive's will. Scores of "president's men" may initial a decision memo or budget figure, so we know the "White House" took action, but the president does not know most of the individuals who initialed it. The object has become to get the "White House" or the "presidency" to approve the decision, rather than to have rational, interpersonal decisionmaking.

There is no way to escape the fact that only people can make decisions. Should the president expect a third-level career staffer in OMB or the White House (who cannot have the knowledge available to a line organization manager) to make a decision more compatible with the president's views than a politically appointed agency head whom the president has, or should have, personally chosen? Is it not easier for the president carefully to choose his top cabinet and agency heads based upon their political loyalty, experience, and expertise, and let them carry out his will while they personally choose their accountable subordinates? Doesn't this make more sense than amassing a staff of several thousand in a centralized White House, most of whom, in an institution like OMB, will be career civil servants without any particular loyalty to the president?

No matter how well the staff is selected in the central staff agencies of the White House, everyone will soon be overburdened. The White House staff can never be as large or as specialized as the line agencies responsible for carrying out policy. Otherwise, the White House staff would be the operating agency. Therefore, necessarily overworked and equipped with a superficial knowledge of the fields they oversee, White House staffers inevitably get in over their heads. But each one is required to make decisions, so he makes them. Or, he delegates to lower-level career staffers, who make decisions in the interest more of "the presidency" than of the president. If the staffer defers to the line officer (this happens more often than not), this delays decisionmaking and often frustrates it. All of this assumes that there are no personal agendas involved. There usually are, and policymaking thus becomes even more chaotic and conflict-driven.

A spectacular example of ingrained superficiality of White House staff decisionmaking occurred over the setting of the Reagan administration's basic policy on personnel reductions. The policy I set was that we should achieve the president's targeted nondefense personnel reductions primarily through attrition, utilize other personnel tools such as furloughs when necessary to achieve budget or personnel reductions, and use layoffs or reductions in force (RIFs)—but only when appropriate and cost-effective. We followed this policy, after publishing it and making it available to OMB, for about three months without incident. When OPM itself became the first to begin making furloughs, problems arose. The national media noticed and, therefore, so did the White House Office.

I was immediately ordered to halt all furloughs and only RIF employees—not only at OPM but throughout the whole government. I hate to ruin my reputation as a tough guy, but I thought it was both needlessly inhumane and politically stupid to fire everyone in sight. Moreover, it would cost almost twice as much as would furloughs. I told the White House messenger so. He demanded a written explanation, and I sent him as full an explanation of our policy as prudence dictated, stressing for his benefit that furloughs were necessary if we were not to increase spending. The next thing I heard was the senior staff ordered me to adopt a RIF-only policy. I refused. Next, I was told officially that Edwin Meese, James Baker, and Michael Deaver personally ordered me to do RIFs only. I refused. Finally, by refusing to budge, I convinced them. In the end, we did reduce non-defense personnel by over a hundred thousand with less than 10 percent RIFed, at the lowest cost, and achieved the president's target. But it took the battle of the century with the very top of the White House to get this simple, obvious policy supported by its staff.

The people in the White House and the agencies spend tons of time trying to communicate with each other. This delays decisions and usually dilutes the decision made to accommodate the number of people involved. Every possible staff structure has been tried to minimize the problem of poor decisions resulting from this process. Every president has tried to manage the impossible. The only solution is to go cold-turkey, to zero out the White House staff. Only this will force the president and the cabinet to deal with political team-making at the top, a task critical to the success of an administration. Then responsibility will be placed where it belongs, in the hands of line officials in the cabinet and subcabinet agencies.

How would a zero-option White House look? The president would set the basic policy in general terms—stronger defense posture with more military spending, and transferring domestic functions to state and local government and the private sector— and some specifics for a limited number of policies in which the president has a personal interest. A story has it that an early OMB director created his "budget" on the back of an envelope after an hour's discussion with the president. That should be the model, not the scores of notebooks and thousands of lines in today's budget. For, the detail rather kills flexibility and decentralized knowledge than gives real control.

After giving broad directions to his agencies, the president would rely upon the cabinet and agency heads. From the White House, the president would use assistants for budget, domestic policy, national security, personnel, congressional affairs, public affairs and communication, and a small cabinet secretariat for coordination purposes. The secretariat would have a half-dozen staffers to keep in communication with the cabinet and the major agencies. The cabinet secretariat would include a personnel office to assist the president in choosing his top executives. The staff of OMB would be removed from the White House complex and merged with OPM and the General Services Administration as a new cabinet management office. Each presidential assistant would have a secretary and, perhaps, one aide.

How would these presidential assistants get their work done without huge staffs? They would be forced to rely upon the political appointees in the agencies. For example, the budget assistant would have to call together all of the chief budget officers in the departments. The congressional affairs assistant would call together the heads of the agency congressional relations offices. Likewise for public affairs and other staff functions. The White House would then be forced to rely upon communication from the line personnel with the expertise, and would have the benefit of many more individuals who have a practical knowledge of the problems to be analyzed. All of this knowledge out in the agencies would be collected by the assistants for the president, but the whole process would take place in the agencies, culminating in the cabinet, whose members would be the president's principal staff and line operating officers.

This makes the cabinet the most important executive institution after the president himself. Yet, this is more in accord with what was originally envisioned and is still generally sanctioned by law. Cabinet government means that the president must personally choose the most capable individuals to fill these positions. And it means they must be political appointees who loyally carry out his policy. And each must choose politically loyal subordinates. If they are not loyal, they should be dismissed.

Cabinet government means that personnel management is recognized as the vital function. The presidential assistant for personnel would be more important, focusing his efforts on building a political team to carry out the agenda the people elected the president to achieve. Its head, like the other White House staff assistants, would be forced to work with OPM and the political assistant secretaries for administration in the departments and agencies to build a political team. It would mean that the president would be the top personnel manager, setting the basic agenda, and then motivating his top political executives, relying upon them to make the government work. His political leadership should inspire their leadership, and so on down the line-management chain to political and career subordinates throughout the government.

I do not see how true reform can result from half measures. Every president and most White House officials and agency heads have found the present system intolerable and inefficient. The only solution is to zero option the White House and to build the president's political and career team on-line in the agencies, for it is much more important to have the loyal members of the team in the line than to have them merely as staff advisers. The line must have the power and the expertise.

Before the Budget and Accounting Act, successful presidents were forced to build around a strong cabinet and the nation was run more efficiently. The weakening of the presidency began with the idea of the centralized presidency. Even the successful administrations since the creation of the welfare-state presidency—in particulars Dwight Eisenhower's—were partially successful because they relied more upon a strong cabinet, a strong and loyal political team in the agencies, and a small White House staff. Our present and future presidents deserve no less than did our earlier presidents, and that means to zero out the White House staff and rely upon the cabinet.

11

Political Administration the Right Way

The major task frustrating good management of the line agencies of the federal government is the Wilsonian myth that government administration is merely a technical task, to be handed over to neutral experts in the bureaucracy or the central management agencies. The myth is a vain attempt to escape human nature and the politics which is its governmental incarnation. The myth is as old as Plato's guardians and the progressive's vision for a neutral civil service, and as new as a recent report by the National Academy of Public Administration.

NAPA, powerful enough to be one of only two congressionally recognized private academies, has long been an advocate of turning government management over to politically "neutral" career bureaucrats. From its first to its most recent report, it has lobbied for fewer political appointees and more power for career officials. A member, a former career civil service director and professor of public admin-

174   REAGAN'S TERRIBLE SWIFT SWORD

istration, has taken the myth to its logical conclusion by
calling for a commission totally independent of the president and the political process to run the bureaucracy.

The myth dominates the graduate schools of public
administration in the United States, which are the source of
a large percentage of the mid- and top-level officials in the
federal bureaucracy. NAPA and the American Society for
Public Administration (ASPA) run training sessions each
year to promote the myth among career officials, who usually attend on government training funds. Their bogeyman
is the political appointee of the president who will bring
politics into government. Imagine that!

The opposing theory of public administration presented
in this book starts first with *The Federalist*'s more realistic
view of human nature, one which says that power is always
a threat to human freedom but that it is intrinsic in government and must rather be controlled by competing institutions than be ignored. Second, as *The Federalist* also
teaches, the theory is republican, in that elections are the
means by which governments and their policies are changed
within that institutional setting. From these two constitutional principles comes a third, more practical one, that
politics necessarily becomes an essential part of internal
government operations, indeed the primary means by which
people can control the instruments of coercion in the
bureaucracy itself.

This theory views government as political because it is
composed of people who have no other discipline within
that single institution than the political relationships between
them. Unlike the private sector, government has no bottom-
line objective measure to provide a "faithful image," as Ludwig von Mises called it, of operations. So, the only possible
substitutions are arbitrary bureaucratic rules or brute force,
and these two do not give a reliable picture—and, in the
case of this theory, developing political networks between
individuals to provide a rough communications substitute.

This political theory of administration has its working
principles too, to guide its network members. *First*, directly

from Mises' insight about the private executive, it follows that a public manager cannot decentralize as can his private counterpart. He himself must know or learn a lot about his political, bureaucratic, and cultural environment. He must be ready and able personally to recognize and respond to any of the many political pressures that can affect his survival. He also must know more about the details of his department than do his peers in the private sector, since in government much of administration is actually policy. If he does not, the political leader will lose control of policy, which is his first responsibility. Unless he has far more detailed knowledge than required of his equivalent in business, he will become a figurehead and turn policy over to those below him. Since the political administrator must delegate less, he must also follow up more.

Second, the political administrator must have a clear understanding of his agenda. He can master details only if he has a clear knowledge of the whole and precisely how policy details fit in and will be implemented. This agenda will be set in the first instance by the program preferences of the president, but must be further developed in every specific policy area by representatives of the president. The political executive must develop this agenda in the spirit in which the president would develop it himself, if the president had the time personally to deal with each of the myriad pieces of government.

Since the president-appointee relationship must be empathetic, the *third* principle requires that the appointee must be politically loyal—often demonstrated through previous work in the election campaign—so that he can develop a detailed program that in truth represents what the president would himself have developed. Also, the appointee must inspire loyalty from his subordinates, and they from theirs.

An administrator must face the fact that his program will be developed in a fishbowl, where all is made public, often prematurely through leaks by hostile political opponents, usually in his own bureaucracy or in the White House. Therefore, the *fourth* principle is for the political executive to ask himself, in each decision and every time he puts something on paper, "How would this look on the front page of the *Washington Post*" (for better or worse)? Calculated propriety is essential to survival of the agenda (and the administrator).

From this follows the *fifth* principle: the political executive must keep his operational agenda close. This is not an attempt to freeze career employees out of policy, as alleged by the NAPA/ASPA public administration community, but simply a matter of preserving the president's agenda as well as keeping the administrator's head from being cut off, whether this involves political foes of the president or career or political subordinates.

The theory's *sixth* principle is that if a political administrator implements the changes in policy promised by the president, he must have the courage to live with the inevitable negative reaction. A porous government bureaucracy will advise the media of any warts and they, in turn, will be pleased to advertise every one of them. The appointee's family and friends will see him splashed all over the newspapers and television screen in a most unflattering light. Since no one can do everything perfectly in an environment of limited delegation, these negatives are an integral part of public policymaking, able to be minimized but not avoided. The only way to avoid criticism is to do nothing. Indeed, this is the favorite tactic of the political opportunist who wants only to survive to advance once back in the private sector, even though he does this at the cost of his only reason for existence as a political appointee, his president's agenda.

The executive who remains a true political administrator must, *seventh*, be confident in the knowledge that he has the legal right to act: he is the boss. American law clearly gives most of the authority to the political appointee and expects him to make the policy decisions under the direction of the president, the checking authority of the Congress, and the courts. It is often difficult to maintain the poise needed for political leadership in the rough-and-tumble environment of Washington, but it is what is legally expected and proper. The bureaucracy is, indeed, obliged in democratic theory and in American law to carry out the orders of the political head, even if this often works better in theory than in practice.

Finally, to maintain poise, the political executive needs these three additional guidelines. *Eighth*, it is easy to become isolated, and therefore important to build friendships with other political appointees who are in the same situation, and to keep friends outside parochial Washington. There is life beyond the beltway, and it is important to visit it to remember that most people are outside of the "gimme" environment of Washington special-interests politics. *Ninth*, other political appointees must be trained to help share the burden of political leadership and, ultimately, to become the leader. For, if he does his job, the original leader will not serve too long. *Tenth*, the political appointee must laugh often at the ridiculous situation he is in, the fishbowl, trench-warfare world of political administration in Washington.

Creating a political administration starts with political executives who understand and have internalized these principles of political leadership. Then, the task of implementing a political public administration is to build the team in a cabinet that extends political discipline throughout the government. It is a task of personnel management: leadership, motivation, teamwork, communication, encouraging excellence, rewarding action, and correcting mistakes.

The president begins by personally choosing the twenty to thirty chief executives who will manage and oversee the major agencies of his government and constitute his real cabinet. His executives must understand and agree with his program, know the subject matter, and follow the ten principles. Above all, these critical leaders must be loyal to the president, or cabinet government through political administration will not work.

The president must take the time himself to create his cabinet team. Unaccountably, most do not. He must review and interview in a detailed way the cabinet and subcabinet executives and White House assistants upon whom his administration will depend. Otherwise, there will be no team and no follow-through on the promises made to the voters during the election. Then the president will give general directions; and, finally, under criteria set by him, he will allow each of his agency heads to choose political subordinates. If the heads are not capable of choosing their own teams, they should not be the heads of the agencies in the first place. Moreover, each agency head will allow his subordinates to do likewise, under the same logic. The assistant for presidential personnel will monitor this process, but not dominate it.

In determining how political appointees should be assigned below the level of major division head, James Watt devised what he called the "rule of three." Into every major subunit of the government organization the agency head sends three political appointees. One must have the leadership skills and knowledge necessary to run the bureau. The second must have the knowledge and administrative competence to see that his superior's orders are implemented. The third needs no technical skills at all. His job, while he is learning, is to make sure that the two others remember why they were appointed by the president in the first place!

Each of the thirty or so cabinetlike agencies of the executive branch will be staffed in this manner. The rule of three will push this model down through several levels of agency organization to each major component of the bureaucracy. The president will give each cabinet head initial instructions and leave him to carry out his program. He will review performance at cabinet meetings. Sound simple? Well, essentially cabinet government is. As President Reagan has said, there are simple solutions if you'll just recognize them.

What about the overlapping responsibilities for programs between agencies? The most obvious answer is to eliminate them, and each new administration should always make an effort to make government organization more rational. Yet, Congress will often oppose rational solutions to save some perk or pork, so a prudent president needs to create councils of the cabinet and subcabinet consisting of the agency heads who share this overlapping responsibility, like those created during the first Reagan administration. But the present theory takes it further. For each program area—environment, civil rights, etc.—the president will choose one person as principal subordinate in that policy area. That person will chair the cabinet council and receive from the president a leading coordinating role over all programs in that area, even those under the organizational purview of another agency head. By assigning a clear "leading minister" role to one responsible person, and a forum to discuss differences, conflicts can be minimized. Abuses of power by the leading ministers will be kept in check by the fact of a collegial, cabinet government where the rest can air disagreements. Ultimately, major disputes will be settled before the president at the cabinet table.

The theory of political administration also embraces the technical principles of a neutral public administration. Fortunately for the Reagan administration, these tools already existed in the Civil Service Reform Act of 1978. The CSRA provides for a technically sound performance appraisal system, which allows conscientious political and career managers to evaluate and communicate effectively with subordinate employees. Although political executives serve at the pleasure of the agency head and can be motivated only through leadership, the CSRA gives the political manager the authority to reward with substantial bonuses those career executives who perform well, to reassign those who need different working environments to be effective team members, and to discipline those who perform poorly. Since being implemented, these essential elements of a sensible personnel administration have been given secure status in Merit System Protection Board and court decisions.

The essential ingredient for a sound theory of political administration is the political will to use this knowledge to implement an administration's agenda. Andrew S. Grove, author of *High Output Management* and president of Intel Corporation, says this same ingredient is critical in private sector management. At bottom, despite critical differences, the essential element in both private and public sectors is courageous leadership. According to Grove, if "we want performance in the workplace, somebody has to have the courage and competence to determine whether we are getting it or not." And, second, after evaluating what is necessary, "we managers need to stop rationalizing and stiffen our resolve and do what we're paid to do," which is "manage our organizations."

Politics being the rougher game, government requires tougher, more courageous leaders held together in a more loyal team. A president can wish to follow personally and order his subordinates to create a political administration, but it is wrong to assume it's easy to find or build the team. That is the real political art of governance, one which can be sought but never perfectly found.

What is certain is that the Wilsonian view of public administration has broken down in America, and in most of the rest of world for that matter. Several European nations, among them the ones who invented the model of Wilsonian administration, requested my assistance for technical advice for shifting to multiple levels of political appointees throughout their government bureaucracies, so they could move their systems closer to ours. Several, including Britain and France, have made some moves in that direction already.

The theory of political administration did have a critical test during the Reagan administration. To the degree it guided action within individual agencies, it seemed to work, placing effective democratic controls upon the bureaucracy. It worked at Interior, it worked at Labor, the Federal Trade Commission, GSA, ACTION, OPM, and many other agencies. But a systematic test of the theory awaits a new administration ready to accept the full challenge of cabinet government.

12

Helping Politicians Say No

Human Nature Likes to Say Yes to Favors

If today's failed government results from overcentralized staff management and overbureaucratized line administration, its root cause is even deeper. For, in the United States, popularly elected representatives keep voting for more and more programs that result in unnecessary, inefficient, and unresponsive bureaucracies. Although the politicians try to persuade us that the people force them to act, public opinion polls do not bear them out. Rather, legislators vote for the programs because too few politicians can say no to organized, relentless, special interests.

Politicians are heavily pressured by interests—other legislators, bureaucrats, contributors, business and union bosses, ideological and social welfare activists, and almost anyone else who wants something special and can afford expensive Washington representation. That's why there are about forty thousand lobbyists and lawyers working in Washington at an average salary of well over $100,000 a year each. And, of course, politicians want things for themselves, including money to ensure their reelection. The only thing that saves the government is that most ordinary people do not ask for anything but good government, or maybe just to be left alone. Still, the army of special interests asks for a great deal. Its Washington representatives are focused, they know the system, they're well paid, *and they never give up* trying to work the system for their special-interest clients.

It is not that politicians are depraved, although some are. Money and crass favor-trading are less important than most people think. Most politicians just do not want to be thought unhelpful—yes by "important" people, but really by anyone. Indeed, most legislators believe that being "helpful" (with other people's money) is their job. It is what makes them feel good as politicians. Besides, they reason that candidates for office who say no too often are not going to be very successful. Yet, as everyone knows, if you say yes to everything, all will be chaos.

We all see this in our own lives, in dealing with our families and friends. When people ask us for something, we like to say yes and give it to them. We do not want to disappoint. Yet, deep down, we know that it is impossible to say yes all the time. Indeed, we know that saying yes to our children can often be the wrong decision and even dangerous for them. We certainly should not say yes to a child who wants to play on thin ice. Even regarding seemingly good things we have to say no; if we don't limit the consumption of candy, our children will get sick. Parents need to set rules. Unless there is some reason to say no, the world is a dangerous, unhealthy, and irrational place.

Saying Yes Is Even Easier in Legislatures

In politics it is even more obvious that the easy thing is to say yes. That is why it is so difficult to create enduring, just, and free governments. And democracies, especially, the philosophers have told us, will perish if representatives cannot say no. Democrats want to do everything: they do not want to say no to any good-sounding idea, especially if they can shift the blame for any bad consequences elsewhere—which in a large government is easy to do because of the difficulty in assigning responsibility. Yet, as with children, governments simply cannot survive on a steady diet of yes. Fortunately, the framers of the American Constitution, unlike most others, recognized the need to "bind government down with the chains of the Constitution"; and it is no coincidence that our regime is also the oldest, most enduring in the world.

It will not do, of course, to ascribe this propensity of saying yes only to politicians. Everyone likes to say yes. Being captured by special interests is less a moral collapse into total depravity, as some modern puritan reformers would have it, than the easy way to get along, "the thing to do."

A former California state senator, H. L. Richardson, tells a story that well illustrates my point. A concerned citizen joins with some local acquaintances to create a movement to make government better, to end favors for privileged groups. His friends work their hearts out and get him elected. On his way to the capital, the legislator dedicates himself to following his principles and not being captured by the special interests. In his first meetings with lobbyists, he is wary and keeps at arm's length. He votes upon principle every time. But the lobbyists are impossible to avoid in the villagelike atmosphere of a capital city, and the representative comes to realize that they are decent people after all. Just like you and me. His daughter becomes friends with one of their sons. His wife gives one of their children a ride to school. He and his wife attend parties with them and become enmeshed in capital social life. Then it happens. The most neighborly lobbyist suggests an amendment that, frankly, makes a lot of sense. The legislator votes for it. But when he goes back home, his former supporters are wrathful. They see his vote as a first step from principle and they fear he is on the way to becoming captured, although they are not quite sure why. The constituents are, in a word, unreasonable over a reasonable vote.

Richardson asks, after the legislator has several such encounters with his constituents—in all of which the legislator understands better than his constituents and is often correct—what does a normal person conclude? The legislator naturally begins to think that his friends and constituents just do not understand the problems. And, of course, to a great extent he is correct: constituents do not know the technicalities of the law (although they know well how to smell a rat). So, inevitably, the legislator is drawn closer and closer to the lobbyists and further from his friends and constituents at home. His lobbyist friends console him, and perhaps schedule a few fundraising events to make up for the loss of financial support from the folk at home. Pretty soon he is isolated from his community, increasingly he is doing the bidding of his lobbyist friends in return for their support, and now feels more "at home" in the capital than in his hometown, which he visits only on campaign swings. The representative becomes part of the capital village establishment, completing a journey many had made before.

Of course, some legislators do not even try to be good. Many see public service as a means to enrich themselves. A small number actually seek or take bribes; but many more see service in Congress as a lucrative career in itself, and the portal to an even richer life afterward. The business of Washington is trading favors, and congressmen are at the apex of the helping profession of the capital. Few of them leave town (if they do) poorer than when they arrived. With excellent contacts to the best lobbying jobs supplementing the world's most generous pension system, saying yes pays handsomely indeed.

How the Founders Tried to Help Human Nature

The great strength of American government is that its founders understood human nature. Rather than pass law after law in a futile effort to eliminate every possible evil, in the mode of modern reformers like Ralph Nader or Common Cause, the framers established certain institutional rules that would neutralize, if not avoid, rather than prohibit bad behavior. They created a government that provided some incentives against congressmen going native and against their human proclivities to say yes to everyone.

The founders required frequent elections for members of the House of Representatives, every two years, expecting that this would keep them close to home and would ensure significant turnover to bring in new blood from the local community every few years, so that long-term relationships within the capital would not develop.

The founders created small districts, to rise to a maximum of thirty thousand people each, so that citizens could know their congressman, keep him advised of constituent concerns, and know if he was misbehaving. Congresses were to meet in the capital city only two or three months a year. Representatives would live at home under the laws they had passed. Congressmen were to be paid little, so that they had to earn their income in their home communities, having to work within the government's red tape (so they would not pass any more laws than absolutely necessary). Districts were to be drawn mostly to clusters of recognizable local communities which would not let their borders be redrawn to the personal advantage of legislators.

But the founders also knew human nature would endure and find ways around even the best institutions. And how far we have come! When former Senate Majority Leader Howard Baker retired a few years ago, he was asked what was the most profound change that had occurred during his career. He, unhesitatingly, said that Congress had changed from a citizen legislature to a Washington bureaucracy.

The reelection rate for members of the House of Representatives is now 98 percent, and the Senate is not far behind. Congress can mobilize eleven thousand full-time patronage partisans, compared with three thousand for the whole executive branch. The average congressman has more than half a million dollars in office budgets, and free use of the mails to generate massive publicity well beyond what is available to opponents. At the same time, campaign finance laws limit the amount of contributions that can be raised by challengers to obtain equal publicity. Even if well-financed opponents arise, congressmen and senators, by the very fact they are in office, get additional free publicity from a now-pervasive mass media relentlessly fed by the congressional "news-making" machine.

Congressional districts are gerrymandered, with the explicit purpose of creatively drawing boundaries to protect incumbents of *both* parties. Districts are so large that representatives, supposed to speak for a half-million people, are known by only a very few and controlled by no one. Most important, Congress meets year round in Washington, with members going home to their local communities only for quick trips on weekends and recesses. With time on their hands in Washington, congressmen try to micro-manage the executive branch—and, without any real knowledge of how agencies operate, further contribute to government's inefficiency.

Even the best congressmen no longer reside in their home communities, identify with or understand their real problems, or live under the laws they themselves impose upon others. The worst are simply out for themselves. Congress has, indeed, changed and become a Washington bureaucracy: fixated on high salaries (now over one hundred thousand dollars per year), long tenure, and pensions even more generous than those of the rest of government—pensions worth more than $3.5 million to the average congressman—and looking forward to a good job lobbying with newly made friends in Washington afterward.

Re-Creating Citizen Legislatures

The founders also gave the people the power to make changes in their government. And as people have realized that Congress has become more bureaucratized and remote, they have become more willing to make the necessary changes. A Gallup poll in early 1990 found that 58 percent of Americans would agree to limit congressmen and senators to twelve years in office. The California Poll found 82 percent in favor of requiring legislators to draw district lines following political, administrative, and topographical boundaries so that a district would represent real communities of interest, instead of being drawn to an incumbent's advantage.

Congress is still required by law to meet for only seven months per year. Congressmen simply suspend this rule each year, but citizens could demand that business be completed each year by the summer. Actually, most of the real legislative business today is done in two or three months. Most of the time is spent looking important, running for reelection, and second-guessing agency decisions. With modern communication and technology, there is no reason congressmen cannot do the needed business between sessions from home, with much less staff, in the manner of many state legislatures. With part-time work, pay can be reduced and with limited terms, pensions can be eliminated, resulting in budget savings. As long as representatives are required to work in their home community and are required to report the sources of their income to their neighbors and competitors, there should be little problem with conflicts of interest from earning a living while in office.

Districts today are just too large. The number of districts in the House of Representatives has stayed the same for sixty years, while the population has multiplied many times. Both the British House of Commons and the New Hampshire legislature are much larger than the U.S. House of Representatives, and there is no reason why the House's seats could not be doubled, or more, to give better representation.

Once Congress has been re-created as a citizen legislature—by limiting staffs, expenses, and benefits; creating fair and smaller districts; limiting the number of terms which can be served; and requiring that congressmen live most of the year in their communities under the laws they pass—Congress still needs additional discipline if it is to say no.

Congress could do well to look to the states to see how they have restrained government's unnecessary and non-productive spending. Indeed, the founders expected that the national government would be reformed over time by the experience in the states, which would act as scores of laboratories to test needed structural reforms. Today, every state in the nation requires a balanced budget, most for many years, to provide the needed fiscal discipline. And, in recent years, more states have been passing laws that put some upper limit on how much government can take from its taxpayers.

As of 1989, thirty states have tried to reform congressional procedures by calling for a constitutional convention to require that the national government have a balanced budget, and to limit the percentage by which Washington's spending could grow each year. This amendment is only four states short of the required two-thirds to force Congress either to pass an amendment by itself or to call a constitutional convention for that purpose.

Long experience in dealing with members of Congress has merely confirmed Aristotle's wisdom that nothing is more important to preserving representative government and freedom than restricting the amount of the people's earnings legislatures may take. Congressmen just cannot stop themselves from seizing money from the very decent and generous American taxpayers—who could spend it better, more humanely—and transferring it to special interests. Despite pressures to restrain it, the government tax take has increased every year but one—that incredibly successful first year of Reagan's tenure— by large increments, even during the Reagan administration.

Some countervailing force needs to be set against this enormous pressure on legislators to say yes. A balanced-budget/tax-limitation constitutional amendment seems the most appropriate means. The founders expected that the natural reluctance of the people to tax themselves would provide this limit—and the existence of a legislative limit to spending growth in the Gramm-Rudman-Hollings Act and the 1990 budget amendments prove public pressure still works—but today the additional protection of a *constitutional* amendment is required to keep a remote Congress under popular control.

It is also necessary to restore the balance of powers set in the Constitution. The founders gave the president the veto, intending that it become the chief means by which the government would say no to Congress's natural appetites. Yet, over the years, clever congressmen have found ways around this by "bundling" many bills together into one, to make it difficult for the president to veto them. They are wise enough to bundle the bills the president believes are needed with wasteful ones, to salve the special interests. On top of this, during the overreaction to the executive excesses of Watergate, the historic recision power—allowing the president the management discretion not to spend every last dollar appropriated for a program if he believed it would be counterproductive—was taken away from the president. By the end of the 1980s, Congress was putting *all* money bills into a single massive bill called a continuing resolution; if the president refused to sign it, the entire government had to shut down. Effectively, the president's constitutional right to veto bills has been stolen from him by clever congressmen.

The president now needs to be given a line-item veto—a power given to three fourths of the states' governors, which would allow him to veto *parts* of bills—or be given at least greater recision power. The purpose is not to dominate Congress but to redress a real constitutional erosion of the president's rights. Congressmen were not given the power—to act as substitute executives. (During the Reagan administration Congress even required a minimum number of employees in an agency when the administrator said they were unnecessary.) The president needs to reach within those massive appropriations bills and excise those elements that are wasteful and unnecessary, and be able to manage his branch.

If congressmen knew their special favors would be exposed to the light of a presidential veto, they might even find time seriously to debate important matters of public policy. They'd still be able to override any veto if a super-majority were convinced it was appropriate. Many are calling for a constitutional amendment to establish a line-item veto, although others—led by Republican Senate Leader Bob Dole—insist that the line-item veto already exists in the Constitution, under the so-called Clause 3 powers of the president. If so, all that would be required is a coura-geous president to exercise that power.

Finally, it is necessary to restore the balance between the national government, the states and localities, and the private sector, a balance expressed best in the Ninth and Tenth Amendments to the Constitution—parts of the Bill of Rights conveniently overlooked by the national government, most presidents, Congress, and the Supreme Court. The Constitution's framers set up a government whereby most domestic problems would be solved by individuals and their families first; then by private enterprise, local charities, and churches; then by community or municipal or county government; then by the state governments; and then, only as a last resort, by the national government. Even to this day, a Gallup poll shows that 80 percent of Americans believe this is the proper order in which to solve problems.

Down to the beginning of the twentieth century, govern-ment was limited, and government meant local govern-ment. The states and national governments spent only one tenth of all tax money between them, largely on the military, the court system, and the vast public lands. Yet, today, gov-ernment regulates almost every area of our citizens' lives, and 57 percent of all government revenues are raised by Washington, and even state revenue exceeds local govern-ment resources.

Clearly, there is an imbalance here, a defect in the way we now rule ourselves. For, historically, vital democratic government has been local government. Being closest to the people, local government is more likely to reflect what people want. Efforts were begun during the Reagan administration to transfer functions back to the private sector and local and state governments—and the national government's share of revenue did decline from 61.7 percent in 1980. But Washington still dominates the process. Today, the people are demanding less government, government more human in dimension and smaller in size. The author's experience with Washington's bureaucracy is that large government is inefficient and impersonal and *unrepresentative*: the major desire within the bureaucracy is usually to stay out of trouble while still obtaining higher budgets and benefits, not helping people whom distant bureaucrats do not even know.

Creating citizen legislatures, restricting spending, redressing the imbalance between Congress and the president, and decentralizing national government by transferring its responsibilities to state and local governments or the private sector, are enormous challenges. Indeed, in many cases the problem is complicated by the fact that the reforms must be legislated by the institution that is the problem itself, Congress.

The smart money says reform cannot overcome the established interests. Yet, imagine the task facing the reformers at the beginning of the twentieth century, to convince United States senators elected by state legislatures that they should be elected by the people directly. Then, every one of the senators had been elected by a legislature and was unsure how well he would do in a direct popular election. The Senate turned down the proposal many times, but with persistence—threatening a constitutional convention and also passing laws in state legislatures requiring direct election—reform prevailed. Why could it not happen again?

13

Political Leadership of the Bureaucracy

The Need to Say Yes to Political Leadership

If it is difficult to get congressmen to say no to the special interests, it is equally challenging to get the political leaders of the executive branch to say yes to their responsibility to implement the president's mandate. All of the incentives in the bureaucratic system are toward caution and not to alter the status quo.

"To get along in Washington, you have to go along" was one of the first pieces of advice I heard when I came to the capital. It is the unofficial motto of the town. Every person who enters the circle of Washington power must deal with its implications. The best way to succeed in, and after leaving, Washington clearly is to follow the advice of the motto. If a person takes a big job in the government and does not upset the special interests or the bureaucracy, there will be no complaints about his tenure. If he spends his time hobnobbing with potential future employers at ceremonial functions, and leaves policy in the hands of the top career executives, they will not leak to the media. The appointee's reputation will be safe so that he will be ready for a bigger job through a better résumé after a short stint in government service. But if all political appointees choose this path, no one will carry out the president's mandate, which by definition usually is to change at least some aspects of policy.

An appointee to the Reagan administration had a clear choice: either follow self-interest and keep a low profile, or gather up some courage and help the president carry out his mandate for change. Many chose the former course and many the latter—some who knew the costs and others who didn't. I was very fortunate to have advantages in making this decision that others did not. I had studied government my whole adult life so did not have the luxury of ignorance which protected some who did the president's will without realizing that alone would put them in the middle of controversy. But I had also lived and worked in the Washington area for a long time before my appointment—even consulting for some congressmen and high-level White House staffers—so that power for its own sake had little allure. I not only had seen those abused by the system who had tried to make changes, but had also seen how those who played it safe had been neutered by their endless compromises.

I have had a very close friend who had worked in a high staff position in the Nixon administration. Tom Charles Huston had carried out (to the extent he was able) a legitimate national security mission for the president and was hounded by the judicial bureaucracy and the media for years afterward. He was harassed for doing a good job, not for any of the illegalities that were committed in those days, and that he opposed. To me, he came out better than his accusers and, especially, better than those who had simply added to their résumés and had achieved nothing of any larger value.

I decided that the need for government reform was great, that Ronald Reagan offered a unique opportunity, and that

I would take the more dangerous path toward the inevitable controversy that would result from giving my all to help accomplish President Reagan's mandate. For there was no doubt in my mind that taking public leadership in cutting the bureaucracy in its company town headquarters would put me in the midst of a firestorm.

To a certain extent, to be a political executive is to take the heat. President Reagan could not have been a successful "teflon president" if his appointees had not deflected some of the fire. By comparison, August 1990 newspaper photographs of a demonstration outside the White House opposing possible furloughs, showed government employee protesters carrying signs critical of George Bush. During the actual furloughs of President Reagan's first term, the signs read, "Dump Devine."

How the Bureaucratic System Frustrates Leadership

How does the bureaucratic system frustrate leadership by a political executive? Its ways are legion, but they all come down to "play it safe." Some examples might help give the reader some of the flavor. But, perhaps, I should begin with an observation from a classic book on the American civil service, *Plunkett of Tammany Hall*, by William I. Riordan.

By his own reckoning, George Washington Plunkett was a statesman. By everyone else's, he was a nineteenth-century ward heeler who reveled in patronage and the other benefits of office. The latter he called "honest graft," to distinguish it from outright theft. His motto was: "I seen my opportunities, and I took em."

One of Plunkett's favorite stories for discussion at his bootblack-stand pulpit started with the battle of San Juan Hill during the Spanish-American War.

After the battle of San Juan Hill, the Americans found a dead man with red hair and blue eyes. They could see he wasn't a Spaniard, although he had on a Spanish uniform. Several officers looked him over, and then a private of the Seventy-first Regiment saw him and yelled, "Good Lord, that's Flaherty." That man grew up in my district, and he was once the most patriotic American boy on the West Side. He couldn't see a flag without yelling himself hoarse.

Now, how did he come to be lying dead with a Spanish uniform on? I found out all about it, and I'll vouch for the story. Well, in the municipal campaign of 1897, that young man, chock full of patriotism, worked day and night for the Tammany ticket. Tammany won, and the young man was determined to devote his life to the service of the city. He picked out a place that would suit him and sent his application to the head of the department. He got a reply that he must take a civil service examination to get the place. He didn't know what these examinations were, so he went all light-hearted to the Civil Service Board. He read the questions about the mummies, the bird on the iron, and all the other fool questions—and he left the office an enemy of the country that he loved so well. The mummies and the birds blasted his patriotism. He went to Cuba, enlisted in the Spanish army at the breakin' out of the war, and died fightin' his country.

That is but one victim of the infamous civil service. If that young man had not run up against the civil service examination, but had been allowed to serve his country as he wished, he would be in a good office today drawin' a good salary. Ah, how many young men have had their patriotism blasted in the same way!

Now, what is goin' to happen when civil service has crushed out patriotism? Only one thing can happen: the republic will go to pieces. Then a czar or a sultan will turn up, which brings me to the fourthly of my argument—that is, there will be hell to pay. And that ain't no lie.

Plunkett called this the "curse of civil service reform." Yet I think it was a bit different from what Plunkett thought. As Plunkett himself noted, reforms have consequences not intended by their proponents. The real curse was that what appeared to be rational rules from the perspective of protecting the bureaucracy, created irrational disincentives for everyone to play it safe.

Early on, when I was told about a deficit in the Federal Employees Health Benefits (FEHB) program, for example, this is how it went. "We are short about a half a billion in the FEHB fund," said the top career executive in charge of this program, "but don't worry about it. We can increase premiums a little this year, ask for a supplemental benefit increase from Congress which we always get, and increase premiums next year again to make up the difference." What political appointee anxious about his reputation would not be tempted to let the bureaucratic experts pass the problem along to the unsuspecting taxpayers and employees and let the problem steal quietly away?

I asked the career staff experts to devise a plan by which we could solve the problem more responsibly. After much cajoling, I was still told we must pass along most of it no matter what we did. But I decided to act anyway. Fortunately, I'd had experience in the health insurance industry in my earlier career and I had studied market economics so I was able to act upon my own knowledge. But the incentive structure of the system itself—certainly at the second refusal to act—would have been to follow the advice of the career executive, using taxes from citizens and insurance premiums from employees to keep the problem out of public view.

If a political manager could expect to get positive recognition for rational economic acts, there might be some incentive to act in the interests of taxpayers. In this case, the reforms we enacted for the health plan saved our employees $300 million and taxpayers a rather substantial $3.6 billion. Indeed, the *Washington Post* did print a favorable editorial on the changes that had been made in the FEHB. But it was well after it could have helped and there was no mention of the reforming political appointee, who had been damned by the employee unions and their allies in Congress through the media for a year. When a charge is made against a government administrator, his name appears prominently in the headlines. If it turns out well, something called OPM (or some other impersonal agency) did it.

If bureaucrats like to avoid problems, interest groups are willing to stir things up. They can afford to since the career and political officials usually bear the burden of the legal and personal scrutiny. One of the first to greet me upon arriving at OPM as head of the transition team was a coalition of health charities concerned that they were not receiving a large enough share of the "undesignated" employee contributions in the government's charitable drive. Under the existing rules, the Combined Federal Campaign charitable drive allowed people to designate funds to certain charities and the remainder, or undesignated, were distributed according to a formula. Half of the funds in the campaign were undesignated, and every charity was interested in how this $50 million was distributed.

As is the case facing new political executives in many areas of policy, the existing political formula made no sense. It was based on historical distributions between different groups and they had been codified into the rules. The health agencies argued that the undesignated funds should be made more fair and current by splitting them according to the same proportion of funds as were designated to charities in each year funds were collected. One was not surprised to learn that the health agencies received the lion's share of the designated contributions. On the other side of the argument, under the historical formula, United Way received over 90 percent of the undesignated funds. If the undesignated funds were split on the basis of the designated contributions, United Way would have its share reduced from $45 million to $22 million, a large loss in income to a not powerless institution.

Business as usual in the bureaucracy dictated that the problem be ignored, or ameliorated in some minor way. But I thought that the existing system was unfair and needed to be reformed—it was a charity after all. I decided to move to a 100 percent designated system. First, I changed the pledge card, which had hidden the designation form under dirty carbon paper, to put the choice of charity up front; second, we made sure that the designated contributions actually went to the charities to which they were designated (they had not previously); and third, we encouraged designations generally. This, naturally, appealed to the health agencies.

But I also set up an organization to administer the campaign for the government, for which United Way in most parts of the country was the reasonable choice. That agency would receive whatever was not designated to any other agency as a payment for administering the fund drive. All donors would be notified, in prominent print, that if they did not designate to a particular charity their contribution would be distributed for them by United Way (or other administrative agency). Although United Way would get a much larger percentage, it was from a much lower undesignated fund total. In fact, the number of designated contributions went up from under 50 percent to over 70 percent of the total. The net effect for United Way was a lower total share—but not a disastrous loss— and the health agencies did get more. More important, a rational policy was created.

The incentives for rational policy in the bureaucracy, however, are few. If a political executive would expect that such an equitable solution would satisfy all, forget it. Contrary to the political science texts, no matter how well group interests are balanced, they all will complain. And they did.

Even if an administrator rules evenhandedly, he will be criticized. Exclude both your conservative friends, such as the National Right to Life Committee and the National Right-to-Work Legal Defense Fund, and you will be accused by a *New York Times* editorial of "harassing" Planned Parenthood by also excluding them. Or Jane Bryant Quinn, in her *Newsweek* column, will say that "Daddy" Devine thinks he knows best for women by picking on Planned Parenthood. In this case the *Washington Post* came to my rescue when I needed it. The timely editorial said that the OPM distinction between traditional welfare and other philanthropic activities was "fair," and that it made sense to focus a charitable drive on the wants of the needy. Even the unions supported me on this. And if the *Post* and the unions backed a political executive, who could be against him? Virtually all the political advocacy groups in the country that wanted a share of the funds they thought they could raise being subsidized by the government's charitable drive.

No program administered by OPM can compare in magnitude or emotion to the Civil Service Retirement System (CSRS). In 1984 CSRS passed unemployment compensation to become the third-largest entitlement program in the whole government; the average benefit paid, when I entered office was $12,000 per year per retiree. Considering the fact that per capita income in the private sector for working was not much higher, and being a political scientist aware of the fact that too generous pensions are poor incentives for good work, I became fascinated with the possibilities of bureaucratic reform and saving taxpayer money at the same time.

The political appointee who reads the textbooks and expects congressmen, as guardians of the public purse, to be allies in saving money does not understand the real incentives in the bureaucratic system he has entered. Once, at an oversight hearing, I marveled out loud at the huge size of the unfunded liability in the employee retirement system (if we had counted it as debt at the time, the then almost one-half trillion would have increased by one half again the total of the whole national debt). To my professed surprise, subcommittee chairwoman Mary Rose Oakar warned me against using this figure; it was not authorized by the CSRS law, which required reporting only a "static" liability not used by any other retirement system in the world but CSRS. She was not impressed with the fact that another, more recent law required that we also report the dynamic liability I had used and was required of the private sector by the government as the only honest one. But the interesting thing was that this congressional leader not only did not expose the problem herself, but was also upset when the political executive even raised the issue.

One reason political executives have little incentive to make changes in government is that policy quickly becomes personal in Washington's villagelike atmosphere, where most of the top actors know each other. I was told by one of the editors of the Baltimore *Sun* that the only talk in Washington when the Reagan administration began its layoffs was a deep shock because the Washington area was supposed to be unemploymentproof. There was great worry that spouses and friends in the government would be dismissed or receive lower benefits, so that changes in policy took on a personal meaning to reporters, lobbyists, congressmen, and other powerful individuals not obviously affected.

On the other hand, he said, there was not much discussion at Washington cocktail parties or even in the Washington media about the two hundred thousand that had been laid off in the automobile industry in the Baltimore area in the past few months. Because the Washington elite were personally involved, even the better reporters could not put the matter in perspective. Actually, the total number of layoffs related to the president's efforts to decrease the size of the nondefense federal work force, was only 11,000 nationwide. This represented four tenths of 1 percent of the federal work force, a percentage that would not even be noticed in the private sector, much less given prominent media attention.

This attitude of protecting friends was very evident when we made our proposal to base government within-grade pay and layoffs more upon performance. *Washington Post* editorial writer Jodie Allen actually told me it was unfair that her friends in the government would have to be rated based upon how they performed in the Reagan administration. She said many of them viewed policy "differently" from the way Reagan did and they should not be expected to perform well under those new policies they opposed— a rather revolutionary principle for government management. When I later announced that a congressional attempt to block our rules was not done properly, her friends in the bureaucracy could not have been disappointed by her editorial that was headed: "OPM to Congress: Drop Dead."

Getting a political executive in trouble with Congress is not a good way to get him to continue to say yes to his responsibilities. However, there is one situation where the system encourages political executives to act; but it is a perverse case. When a political executive is leaving office there is a great incentive to do something that will do him some good when he gets back in the private sector. Take the civil service examinations Plunkett was so concerned about. The Professional and Administrative Career Examination (PACE) did not quite have the mummies and the birds anymore, but it was close. It still hired upon Plunkett's hated merit, rather than upon good old patronage. Yet, as noted above, PACE is as dead today as the mummies; and patronage—not political, but bureaucratic—reigns in the civil service.

PACE was killed by a departing Carter administration Department of Justice political executive ingratiating himself with his new associates in the private sector, who thought the exams were discriminatory. The departing political executive did not burden his outside friends with the financial costs and effort of proving their case in the courts, thereby certainly earning their good will—which counts for cash on his Washington favor bank balance sheet when he reenters the lobbying world of the nation's capital.

At least Plunkett would understand the incentives involved in this modern form of honest graft (within the Department of "Justice" no less); and he must be pleased to be vindicated by the Republic's getting rid of those hated exams that had the nerve to hire and promote in the bureaucracy based upon merit.

The System Catches Up

For two years (longer than the eighteen-month historical tenure for a political appointee), I was able to act against the perverse incentives protecting the status quo, changing personnel policies that had previously been impervious to reform. Then things started catching up. As mentioned above, opponents of my reforms, primarily among the careerists at OMB, were hurting my effectiveness with

Congress by leaking reports published in the media that my reforms did not have the support of "the White House." Although I did have that support, getting it acknowledged publicly was another matter, with everyone protecting the president from any controversy. So I embarked upon the risky strategy of forcing the smart guys' hand.

My ploy of holding the dramatic press conference, with the eleven thousand postcards, did work to force a statement from a high White House official and temporarily ended the weakening of my support. But the cost was high. As the reporter Tom Diaz had noted, it was only a question of time until my string would end. I had decided to resign if the ruse did not work and now determined to get as much accomplished as possible each day until my luck ran out. It was amazing that it lasted almost two more years, when my term ran out.

The director of OPM was one of the few top executive positions with a set term, which fact required that I be reconfirmed by the Senate. The director had been given a set term so that he could not be improperly pressured by the president, but the effect was to ensure that active incumbents would not be able to win renomination. John Harrington, the assistant to the president for presidential personnel, told me to prepare for a secretarial appointment the second term; but a series of Byzantine maneuvers, which ended with him in the cabinet, left me to be reappointed at OPM, which we all realized would be difficult politically.

I should have realized the string had played out, that I was in a no-win position. By now, the nomination was late and if hearings were delayed, support would erode from senators who would support me only if no additional controversy emerged. The problem was that I would be out of office and the White House did not trust Loretta Cornelius, the deputy director of OPM (who had earlier publicly disparaged the president). So, the White House wanted me to continue in operational control—limited only by her formal legal authority—without the real power. Even with these impediments, it looked as if I would win enough

Democratic support to offset the two likely Republican defectors (who represented large federal employee constituencies) so that delay would not become a problem. Then the fates sealed the day.

Post columnist Mary McGrory incorrectly reported the Sunday before the hearings were to take place that I had made disparaging remarks about Senators Ted Kennedy and Pat Moynihan at a dinner that Friday. Although she made a correction on Monday, the damage had been done. Democratic senators were meeting that very weekend, and they decided to teach this wise guy a lesson and closed ranks against my confirmation. It was all over but the spectacle of throwing the director to the lions.

To meet the impossible demands of protecting the White House from my deputy and protecting myself from a legal challenge from her, I drew up a series of legal papers before my term expired giving my new position second rank to the deputy, with authority to act in her stead unless she objected. While this protected me legally, it left me exposed to political criticism for taking too much power if the nomination lingered, which it now did for weeks. At this point, several opponents in Congress threatened the deputy for not exercising control of OPM. Although she had signed the cover papers effectuating the arrangement, she had not understood them (and, frankly, I did not expect that she would); and she now turned upon and dismissed me, after the lack of confidence in her by the White House implied by the documents had been explained to her.

The White House stood by my nomination, but there was little doubt it would fail. It was too late to get out gracefully so I decided to fight to the end, even though I now heard that Cornelius would testify that I told her to lie to Congress about our arrangement. As it turned out at the nomination hearing, when she was asked directly if I told her to lie, she refused to use the term. She simply repeated that I said she could tell Congress she had signed the cover document and that implied understanding the rest. The final hearings were dramatic, with me defending my record and actions, in the opinion of most of the media at the hearing, successfully. But it was the end; I did not have the votes on the committee, so I asked the president to withdraw my nomination and he did so with deep regret.

Will There Be Another Don Devine?

"Will we see another Don Devine anytime soon?" asked the president of the U.S. Chamber of Commerce, Richard L. Lesher, in his nationally syndicated column after the nomination battle.

"If you as a government official intend to do what the American people want you to do—and you have to step on the toes of the denizens of the iron triangle of Congress, the federal bureaucracy, and interest groups in the process—woe betide you. No effort will be spared, and no stone unturned, to keep you from accomplishing your goals," said Lesher. "Instead of reaping the due reward for his efforts, Dr. Devine became the latest victim of a form of Washington trench warfare."

A few days after my withdrawal, Assistant Attorney General William Bradford Reynolds was denied confirmation for a promotion to associate attorney general. Others later followed down the same path. A political executive would have to be deaf not to get the message: don't make waves; don't try to change things. But I had; and the system had caught up. Was it worth the cost?

Over the four years of my service, I had radically transformed OPM, a major agency itself with the fourth-largest budget authority in the government. We had cut personnel by 25 percent (19 percent in standardized work-years) and were performing essentially all the same functions, faster and at lower unit cost by every measurable indicator. Before we reduced personnel, too many people literally were bumping into one another and causing inefficiencies. With fewer employees, more work could get done.

OPM was also a leader in the area of reducing waste and fraud. By increasing management controls on pension payments to reduce overpayment, we saved $3 million; and in matching our CSRS files with those of other agencies to catch ineligibles, we saved over $2 million. By simplifying the check refund policy, we saved almost $1 million. Audits led to management savings in the millions. Backlogs of retirement checks were ended. Before our administration, early retirements in situations where employees were being laid off were given without proof that layoffs would actually take place. By insisting upon such proof, including a cost-benefit analysis, we saved $160 million over four years. Although each of these reforms may sound like chicken feed in the Washington world of billions, administrative savings alone at OPM—in one modestly sized agency over its five-year budget cycle—totaled $964 million.

It was in the area of governmentwide reforms, however, where I made my major fiscal impact. Early in my term I saw from the data (certainly someone must have noticed before) that *one third* of the government's retirements were on disability. Now there are some government employees who jump out of airplanes at 500 feet, but most sit safely behind a desk and shuffle papers. Even a 5 percent rate would be high, and we had 32 percent retiring on disability! I discovered our definition dated back to the 1940s and it implied that one had to be healthier to go back to work than he or she was before the "disability." Further, we required very little proof even of this.

By requiring proper proof—"a note from your doctor"— that there actually *was* a disability and by changing the definition of disability to that used in the Rehabilitation Act, early retirements were reduced by an incredible 58 percent. This was done without any complaints from employees. I was even named public Handicapped Employer of the Year by the District of Columbia Rehabilitation Association. These efforts saved taxpayers $1.2 billion, and $4.9 billion over the five-year budget cycle.

An additional $2 billion was saved in miscellaneous other pension reforms, not counting the tens of billions to be saved ultimately by the fact that the Reagan administration was able to place new federal employees in a new lower-cost retirement system integrated with social security. The total savings to the taxpayer from the health insurance reforms in the FEHB program previously mentioned were $13 billion over the following five-year budget cycle.

Some of the accomplishments were less able to be quantified, but no less important. We were able to implement the new performance management system authorized by Jimmy Carter's Civil Service Reform Act (CSRA). I even sought to extend these reforms, as provided in the act, by proposing regulations to expand pay for performance to the rest of the work force, proposals still working their way through the system. Most important, through CSRA's authority, we brought government under the control of its political executives. As Paul Taylor, in a series on the bureaucracy for the *Washington Post*, noted, "The Reagan administration has moved more aggressively, more systematically, and more successfully than any in modern times to assert its policy control over the top levels of its bureaucracy." Princeton University professor Richard P. Nathan likewise has noted the effectiveness of the Reagan administration in "grabbing hold" of personnel.

The bottom line for my four years as director of OPM is that I saved more than $6 billion directly over my four years, cumulating to $20 billion over the five-year budget cycle—more than the fiscal year 85 budgets of the Department of Housing and Urban Development and the Department of Commerce combined—and made many efficiency reforms. Even some from the opposition party were kind enough to recognize the job done. Democratic Senator William Proxmire said, "There is no question that Dr. Devine has done a good job of holding down the cost of his agency's operations." One employee association head—who wears a Democratic tie pin—said, while disagreeing with my policies, "I'll give him credit, though. He is one of the most effective directors I've ever seen, and I've been around for forty years."

The *Wall Street Journal* said I was "a vigorous and able man who wants to prove government can be managed," one who was "effective." The *Detroit News* said I was "one of President Reagan's most effective 1981 appointees." The *Richmond News Leader* said I was "the most qualified person ever to run the civil service." The president said he was "very proud" of my accomplishments.

Was it worth it? You bet it was. I enjoyed a deep sense of accomplishment, I probably saved more billions than any other appointee, I helped build the effective team that implemented President Reagan's reforms, and I had a great experience which I relished every minute.

But this does not deal with Lesher's question, "Will we see another Don Devine anytime soon?" The answer is probably not; at least not until another Reagan or New Deal movement committed to fundamental reform is forged. Too efficient a government does upset the iron triangle and it will exact such costs that few will be willing to bear them except in a great cause. In a perverse way, this has its satisfaction: as the astute Professor Nathan has noted, how can liberals ask for a larger welfare state if the present one cannot be run efficiently? And it is clear from my experience that government and its associated interests will resist efficient management to the death. And that means the welfare state is moribund too.

The Reagan administration tried to reduce government power and was only partially successful. But it also did something else just as important. It proved that free men and free institutions—outside the power domain of government—work more efficiently than the national government welfare state. Private companies and associations in free markets work, and government does not, even when extraordinary efforts of leadership are applied against the incentives not to act. Indeed, the economy was turned around when all the administration really did was set the private sector more free of government. While markets will work, interest groups will frustrate government performance; and interest groups, including those associated with the bureaucracy, are an intrinsic element of government.

My four years taught me in the most direct way possible that the welfare state is a mirage. It cannot work. A sensible political management can make gains, but interest groups will win concessions in the long run from a pliant Congress and a willing bureaucracy, and that will doom efficient operations. The bureaucracy and Congress will first and foremost protect their own interests, frustrating reforms that could make government more productive.

The bureaucracy successfully protected its own interests against some Reagan administration efforts for further reform. But the bureaucracy lost the war. For government reform will go on—and has during the Bush administration—even if at a reduced level of intensity. Much more important, the real proof the bureaucracy lost is that no one looks to national government for the efficient provision of genuine welfare any longer. The future will look to the private sector or local government. And that fact means the Reagan revolution was successful and more than worthwhile, especially for those fortunate enough to serve as political appointees in the administration.

The Eternal Problem of a Mandarin Class

Throughout the nineteenth century, one of the most unusual aspects of American society—one that amazed European observers—was the small size of national government bureaucracy in the United States compared to those in other nations. As late as 1900, government spent a small fraction of GNP and 90 percent of these expenditures were local. It was not until American involvement in World War I that the first large national bureaucracy in the United States was created.

Although Presidents Warren Harding and Calvin Coolidge attempted to cut it back in size to prewar "normalcy," Woodrow Wilson had created a bureaucratic machinery that could resist enough of their efforts to endure until a more favorable president came along. More important, Wilson had given it a philosophy to legitimize its control, one accepted even by the administration of Republican President Herbert Hoover. With the rise of the New Deal under Franklin Roosevelt in the 1930s, big government and big bureaucracy became a central part of American life.

Surveys from the 1930s show that these programs were not demanded by a majority of the people nor, in most cases, did specific policies have even popular majority support. Some demands came from those who truly wanted to help the needy. Other demands came from economic interests that expected to benefit from government funding. But many political science studies suggest that *much of the demand for more government action came from the bureaucracy itself.*

This makes sense. The more power and prestige of government, the more important is the bureaucrat who works for it. The more people working under the supervision of the bureaucrat, the more important the latter's position and the more highly he is paid. Indeed, in most cases, success in the bureaucracy depends upon building empires. And those who rise to the top are those who are best at serving their supervisor's interest in building that pyramid beneath them without creating enemies in other bureaucracies—not those who are best at serving the people or most considerate of their liberties. It is not so much, as F.A. Hayek thought, that the worst rise to the top, as that those who can best build the bureaucracy to their supervisor's satisfaction, and look as if they are working without making waves, rise to the top.

The power center of today's national career bureaucracy rests within the permanent staff of the Office of Management and Budget (OMB), in the other clearance-approval central offices, especially in the Department of Justice, and in the senior career executive positions in the agencies. Incumbents of these positions have been in the government long before political administrations arrive and remain long after they leave; they are the permanent executive branch, independent of any particular president or Congress.

These structures are reinforced by budget, legal, personnel, and other administrative bureaucracies within each agency, all of which keep in touch with each other through their OMB "oversight" officer. At the apex of the power structure is the "iron triangle" of personal relationships that develop between the top members of the permanent staffs of OMB and agencies, congressional subcommittee staffs, and special-interest representatives (including the media).

The supreme power of bureaucracy is to exercise authority, to impose it's will. Whether the motivation is good or ill, the satisfaction of directing national or world events is exhilarating. With one third to one half of all economic activity in the United States today directly under the command of its bureaucracy—and almost everything else indirectly affected—that power is enormous. But the exercise of that power in recent years has been proved wanting, essentially breaking down in the stagflation economic crisis under Jimmy Carter in 1980.

Through it all the bureaucracy was doing fine, consolidating control over its internal mechanisms, especially promotions. As noted, by the 1980s most of the power positions in the government were filled through so-called name requests rather than through merit selection. Name requests are made by career executives and managers to reward those who do what their career leaders tell them; it is a bureaucratic version of the spoils system. Having control over one's subordinates future is heady stuff indeed, flattering to the will and the currency of internal power relations.

The frills of bureaucracy for the careerist in the federal government today make up for the burdens of perpetual flattering necessary to move up. The physical size of government offices for middle-level executives and managers astounds most private executives. The amount of staff available to serve the government executive is far larger than that in the private sector. And there are opportunities for free travel, vacation spots for "training," the longest personal vacations known to man—up to six weeks—and other such benefits of office not available to most in the private sector.

American bureaucrats are also nicely rewarded in material benefits. As noted, salaries are competitive— even to the advantage of the government employee, except at the very top—and compare to the private sector's. Whatever may be given up on salary, however, is more than made up by federal civil service retirement, the most generous pension in the world. The average private business spends about 17 percent of payroll on retirement and social security— that half of the private sector which can afford pensions at all. On a current cash basis the federal government spends about 33 percent of payroll—almost 100 percent more—to retire its bureaucrats happily.

But this does not represent the true value of the retirement system as a perk to the bureaucracy. Calculating the government payments on the same basis as required by the government for the private sector, the government spends about 85 percent of its payroll on retirement. This is wildly in excess of personnel compensation in business. The cost of this bureaucratic reward system to society is monumental: only Medicare and social security cost more, and they help a hundred times as many people. The average federal career executive more than makes up for his salary by receiving over a million dollars in retirement benefits, compared to an average $375,000 over a lifetime for a comparable executive in the private sector.

Federal bureaucrats are a favored class, a mandarin class, with salary and benefits well beyond those available to the overwhelming number of citizens they oversee. At the top are millionaires on retirement benefits alone, with impregnable job security and colossal power. No wonder the bureaucracy resists when an administration tries to limit its powers and perquisites. All of these perks combine to isolate the top-level decisionmaking bureaucrats from the challenged lives of average citizens. They are not evil individuals, but such isolation makes them insensitive to peoples' needs, so that they become unable to recognize even when they trample upon the citizens' liberties.

The Need for Courageous Political Leaders

Americans are fortunate that the powers of their mandarin-class bureaucracy are restricted and the abuses limited when compared to those in other countries. Power remains divided and leaders are selected through elections. And, through these elections, the voters can demand that bureaucracy be reduced and its mandarin proclivities reined in. The voters did give the Reagan administration such a mandate. By restraining taxes, spending, and regulations, and by implementing a political theory of administration, the Reagan appointees attempted to further that tradition of restricting bureaucracy's power over peoples' lives.

Institutional constraints such as balance of powers between the branches and division of powers between the levels of government are undoubtedly the most important part of what has made America successful—having the same constitution longer than any other country in the world. But, as the founders noted, without a virtuous people any institutional arrangement will fail. This is especially true for the people who serve in government.

For, politics is people. As noted before, it is necessary for Congress to have members with the courage to resist special interests. Yet, congressmen are not in the position to oversee the vast number of things the bureaucracy does; there is just too much to see and congressmen and their staff are too far away to see it. Nor can the courts, which, like Congress, can only act afterward. If a country is to avoid a mandarin bureaucracy insensitive to the peoples' liberties, much of the oversight must be placed in the hands of political executives. If those executives are courageous enough to do their duty, and if the citizenry gives them support to persist in that work, many of the historical excesses of a mandarin-class bureaucracy can be avoided.

The overwhelming number of people in the American bureaucracy are good, decent people. It is not the people but the bureaucratic system they work under. Most will accept determined political leadership and do their job. It is not their fault if normal bureaucracy takes over, but that of the political executive who fears to exercise his authority. Indeed, the universal complaint of average government workers is the iron-handed, arbitrary, and self-promoting rule of their career supervisor. They eagerly accept political direction as a liberation from the normal bureaucratic game which tyrannizes them. They much prefer productive work and its rewards, even when they do not agree with the political agenda. Certainly, that was the case at OPM.

The problem of motivating people for good government is as old as the human condition. As the politically astute Edmund Burke said when the United States was in its infancy, "The only thing necessary for the triumph of evil is for good men to do nothing." Or as Calvin Coolidge, that most commonsense American of all the presidents, put it:

> Nothing in the world can take the place of persistence. Talent will not; nothing is more common than unsuccessful men with talent. Genius will not; unrewarded genius is almost a proverb. Education will not; the world is full of educated derelicts. Persistence and determination alone are omnipotent. The slogan "press on" has solved and always will solve the problems of the human race.

Doing nothing or persisting in his duty is the challenge facing every citizen and especially each political appointee. Whether the appointee accepts his mission will determine to a great degree whether America will remain free or go the way of ancient China, ruled and then ruined by a mandarin class only interested in its own perquisites.

Persistence for what? Not everyone will agree with the mission Ronald Reagan set; but everyone can recognize that his administration was given a popular mandate to change from the existing welfare state. As President Reagan saw it, the mandate was to restore freedom and federalism as the founders understood it. Although his administration did not achieve all it set out to accomplish, it did have a limited success in pruning back the powers, perquisites, and controls of the centralized bureaucracy;

even in returning some functions to the private sector and local government.

Although total government spending actually increased from 22.6 to 24.8 percent of GNP for the first six years of the Reagan administration, political scientists Mark S. Kamlet, David C. Mower, and Tsai-tsu Suy have shown that, "by cutting taxes and 'starving the budget,' Reagan shrank total spending by about $50 billion by fiscal 1986—or by $94 billion for the entire 1982-86 period—below the levels that would have prevailed under his predecessors."

More important to the Reagan goal of reducing domestic national government, over the whole period of the Reagan presidency from FY 1982 to FY 1989, nondefense spending decreased from 17.9 to 16.4 percent of gross national product (even total spending as a percent of GNP decreased to 22.3 percent). The size of this decline can only be appreciated by noting that President Bush's nondefense spending increased from 16.4 to 19.8 percent of GNP only two years after Reagan's departure—a *$170 billion* overall dollar increase.

Most important, "controllable" domestic outlays and the size of the nondefense bureaucracy were reduced absolutely—not merely relatively—for the first two revolutionary years. This was an accomplishment of no little historical moment, even if insufficient to claim that bureaucracy had been routed.

At one of my last cabinet meetings, I reported that the administration was losing some ground in its plans to reduce the bureaucracy. After I completed presenting the data, President Reagan began to wax philosophical. While asking his cabinet and staff to redouble their efforts to reduce nondefense employment, he emphasized how difficult that would be. The president said, in his reading of history he was not aware of any nation that had turned back from bureaucratic statism after having gone as far as had the United States. But, characteristically, he was optimistic, hopeful that America could escape the stultifying welfare state. "Although no country has come back," he winked, "I would like us to be the beginning; I would like us to be the first."

That sounded like a worthwhile goal then; and it still does.

Index